OECD Territorial Reviews

Delineating Functional Areas in All Territories

This work is published under the responsibility of the Secretary-General of the OECD. The opinions expressed and arguments employed herein do not necessarily reflect the official views of OECD member countries.

This document, as well as any data and map included herein, are without prejudice to the status of or sovereignty over any territory, to the delimitation of international frontiers and boundaries and to the name of any territory, city or area.

Please cite this publication as:
OECD (2020), *Delineating Functional Areas in All Territories*, OECD Territorial Reviews, OECD Publishing, Paris, *https://doi.org/10.1787/07970966-en*.

ISBN 978-92-64-84696-8 (print)
ISBN 978-92-64-76747-8 (pdf)

OECD Territorial Reviews
ISSN 1990-0767 (print)
ISSN 1990-0759 (online)

Photo credits: Cover © iStock/Getty Images Plus.

Corrigenda to publications may be found on line at: *www.oecd.org/about/publishing/corrigenda.htm*.
© OECD 2020

The use of this work, whether digital or print, is governed by the Terms and Conditions to be found at *http://www.oecd.org/termsandconditions*.

Foreword

Amid heightened attention on growing geographic inequality, various OECD member countries have re-oriented their regional development policies towards a place-based approach to foster spatially inclusive economic development. In supporting this objective, the OECD Regional Development Policy Committee (RDPC) has highlighted the need for timely, accurate and informative territorial indicators in order to both design and monitor policies. Effective regional development policy not only requires subnational indicators for different territorial units such as regions, cities or rural areas, but also entails the recognition of economic linkages that exist between different territories. In particular, local labour markets extend beyond administrative borders and create functional linkages across areas. With respect to a functional definition of space, most OECD countries have focused their work on larger cities and their surrounding area of economic influence by establishing the concept of functional urban areas. However, functional areas such as integrated local labour markets exist across a country's entire national territory. Extending this concept to non-urban areas can help policy makers analyse subnational developments and design spatial policies that are better targeted to intermediate and rural areas.

Functional Areas for All Territories provides a comprehensive review of existing approaches to delineating functional areas across countries' entire national territory as a tool for territorial statistics and regional policy making. The report outlines the rationale and value added for functional territories as a complement to established administrative geographies. It explains and discusses the most important challenges and methodological aspects of delineating functional areas based on travel-to-work commuting flows or novel sources of data. Finally, the report develops a set of methodological guidelines for identifying functional areas. In applying these guidelines in five OECD countries, the report demonstrates the feasibility of delineating functional areas across diverse types of country geographies in a consistent manner.

This report contributes to the work programme of the OECD on regional development and territorial statistics. It was approved by the Working Party on Territorial Indicators (WPTI) and the RDPC on 9 November 2019.

Acknowledgements

This report was produced by the OECD Centre for Entrepreneurship, SMEs, Regions and Cities (CFE), led by Lamia Kamal-Chaoui, Director, as part of the programme of work of the Regional Development Policy Committee (RDPC). The review was made possible by financial support from Statistics Canada.

The OECD would like to thank the members of the project's scientific committee for their valuable comments, feedback and guidance throughout the project: Alessandro Alasia and Peter Murphy (both Statistics Canada), Luisa Franconi (Istat), Valeriya Angelova and Teodora Brandmueller (both Eurostat), Ksenia Shadrina (US Economic Development Administration) and Siiri Silm (University of Tartu).

Alessandro Alasia, Anne Munro and Peter Murphy (Statistics Canada) provided extensive feedback on an earlier draft of the report and pursued the mapping exercise based on Python in Canada and the United States. Luisa Franconi made detailed comments and provided important advice on both the methodological guidelines as well as the experience of Eurostat and Istat with functional areas. Siiri Silm generously shared the aggregated mobile phone flow data and helped draft the parts on the Estonian experience by using novel data to identify territorial linkages. Julia Schmitt-Schulte (Statistics Netherlands) provided input and data for cross-border functional areas in Europe. Finally, the OECD thanks Professor Mike Coombes for providing substantive feedback and offering detailed comments on the report.

The report was prepared by Lukas Kleine-Rueschkamp (Chapters 1, 2, 3, 4, and 6) and Milenko Fadic (Chapters 4 and 5). It was co-ordinated by Lukas Kleine-Rueschkamp and Paolo Veneri, and overseen by Rudiger Ahrend, Head of the Economic Analysis, Statistics and Multi-Level Governance Section. Pilar Philip prepared the review for publication.

Table of Contents

Foreword 3

Acknowledgements 4

Executive summary 9

Chapter 1. Why delineate functional areas in all territories? 11
    Functional and administrative geographies 12
    Better data for all territories: A statistical perspective 14
    Better policy design, delivery and evaluation for all territories 16
    Notes 17
    References 18

Chapter 2. Main approaches and challenges in defining functional areas 19
    Core-flow-based versus multidirectional-flow-based 20
    Geographic building blocks 22
    Approaches without mobility flow data 24
    Specifications and sensitivity 24
    Challenges in analysing and integrating outputs 25
    Notes 26
    References 26

Chapter 3. The current experience of OECD countries 27
    Survey of OECD countries 28
    Examples of policy application in OECD countries 29
    Detailed country examples of functional areas 30
    Notes 42
    References 42

Chapter 4. Methodological guidelines to define functional areas 45
    A multidirectional-flow and bottom-up iterative process 46
    The importance of parameter selection 47
    Transparency through open source 50
    Consultation or user feedback 51
    Notes 51
    References 51

Chapter 5. Applying existing methods to countries without established functional areas 53
    Canada 55
    United States 57
    Mexico 59
    Korea 61
    Estonia 63
    Note 64

References 64
Conclusion 65
Annex A. Country examples: EU country delineations of functional areas 67
Annex B. Methodological algorithms 71
Distances from success 71
Search strength 71
Annex C. LabourMarketAreas – R package 72
An example of an LMA delineation process 72
Notes 75
Annex D. Self-contained labour areas (SLA-ZTA) – Python package 76
Annex E. Sensitivity of functional areas to parameter specification 79

Tables

Table 5.1. Summary of results 54

Table A E.1. Sensitivity analysis, Canada 79
Table A E.2. Sensitivity analysis, United States 80
Table A E.3. Sensitivity of results excluding FUAs, Mexico 81
Table A E.4. Sensitivity analysis, Estonia 82
Table A E.5. Sensitivity analysis, Korea 83

Figures

Figure 1.1. Mismatch of municipal boundaries – Paris and Rome 13
Figure 2.1. Core-based and multidirectional-based functional areas 21
Figure 2.2. Comparison of core- and multidirectional-flow based approaches 22
Figure 3.1. WPTI survey on the use of functional areas 29
Figure 3.2. Functional areas in the UK: 2011 travel to work areas (TTWAs) 33
Figure 3.3. Functional areas in France 35
Figure 3.4. Italian LMAs 37
Figure 3.5. LMAs without cross-border information: Belgium, the Netherlands and North Rhine-Westphalia 38
Figure 3.6. LMAs with cross-border information: Belgium, the Netherlands and North Rhine-Westphalia 39
Figure 3.7. City centres, urban areas and their economic area of influence in Estonia 41
Figure 4.1. Steps to create functional areas 47
Figure 4.2. Self-containment requirements for functional areas 48
Figure 5.1. 2016 Census metropolitan areas (CMAs), 2016 census agglomerations (CAs) and 2016 census subdivisions (CSDs), Eastern Canada 56
Figure 5.2. 2016 Census metropolitan areas (CMAs), 2016 census agglomerations (CAs) and self-contained labour areas (SLAs), Eastern Canada 56
Figure 5.3. Functional areas (FAs) in the United States 57

Figure 5.4. Functional areas (FAs) and functional urban areas (FUAs) in the United States 58
Figure 5.5. Functional areas (FAs) in Mexico 59
Figure 5.6. Functional areas (FAs) and functional urban areas (FUAs) in Mexico 60
Figure 5.7. Functional areas (FAs) in Korea 61
Figure 5.8. Functional areas (FAs) and functional urban areas (FUAs) in Korea 62
Figure 5.9. Functional areas (FA) in Estonia 63
Figure 5.10. Functional areas (FA) and functional urban areas (FUAs) in Estonia 64

Figure A A.1. Labour market areas in Hungary 67
Figure A A.2. Experimental labour market areas in Finland 68
Figure A A.3. Labour market areas in Bulgaria 69
Figure A A.4. Labour market areas in Portugal 70
Figure A C.1. Scheme of the implementation of the R package LabourMarketAreas 73
Figure A D.1. Scheme of the computational flow implemented by the Python package SLA-ZTA 77

Boxes

Box 1.1. OECD territorial classification 15

Executive summary

Effective policy design requires sound statistical evidence on socioeconomic trends. For regional policy makers, such evidence needs to reveal information on differences in socioeconomic outcomes across space. Therefore, having granular data and indicators on relevant geographies is of paramount importance to regional policy. In order to design, implement and monitor effective regional development policy, it is crucial that such policy addresses the right geographic scale.

National statistical offices (NSOs) need to produce statistical indicators at a spatial detail that captures the socioeconomic geography of countries as well as being useful to policy makers. Most of the subnational geographies used by NSOs to collect and/or publish statistical indicators correspond to the units of the administrative organisation of countries, such as regions, provinces or municipalities.

However, such administrative geographies are not always the most appropriate or suitable scale to inform policy makers, nor are they able to capture how socioeconomic trends differ across space. This creates a common challenge for policy makers and statistical institutes alike. Both types of actors rely on statistical information based on administrative geographic units, even though people's everyday lives and economic realities do not exclusively take place within such administrative units. Instead, economic linkages often connect people from different municipalities, towns or regions.

Policy makers need to look at the economic organisation of the territory to pursue policies at the right scale, especially when it comes to issues such as service provision or international comparability. Therefore, functional areas can complement administrative areas as a unit of analysis or the target of policy making. In recognising the importance of economic linkages, policy makers also need to realise that economic and social realities, which might once have been the rationale for establishing an existing administrative structure, change over time and thus territorial linkages between different areas might evolve.

The tool and concept of functional areas are increasingly used in efforts to capture the socioeconomic interactions at a local level and to respond to policy challenges in an effective manner. Per definition, a functional area or functional region is a territorial unit that results from the structure of social and economic relations between residents across space. Its boundaries do not necessarily reflect administrative geographies or historical events. Consequently, a functional region offers an alternative subdivision of territories. The foundation for economic and social relations ensures that functional areas capture human behaviour and thereby typically offer a better reflection of individuals' daily lives.

Despite their policy relevance, numerous countries remain without any clearly identified functional areas. In other countries, functional areas are often limited to cities and their area of economic influence (functional urban areas), even though territorial linkages exist in all types of territories, rural and urban areas alike. In addition, the delineation of functional areas, where it exists, varies across countries due to methodological differences. At the same time, new and emerging data sources provide novel alternatives to traditional methods for delineating functional areas and could thereby support their increased use in OECD countries.

All those reasons highlight the need for a comprehensive review of the approaches used to map out functional areas in OECD countries. This report offers such a review without imposing statistical conventions on member countries. It discusses the rationale for mapping functional areas across all territories, beyond metropolitan areas. It presents the prevailing approaches to define functional areas in OECD countries, explains the main methodological aspects and challenges, describes the type of data sources used, and summarises the respective implementations. Furthermore, it identifies methods to harmonise or compare, where possible, functional areas across OECD countries. The report also presents evidence of novel approaches to delineating functional areas based on new sources of data, which might constitute an alternative in the absence of commuting data. Finally, the report proposes a number of methodological guidelines and applies them to map functional areas in five OECD countries, where those geographies do not exist.

In pursuing these objectives, the report demonstrates the relevance of functional areas as a tool for the design of regional development policy. It provides extended coverage of functional areas across several OECD countries and offers a methodological guide to delineate functional areas under different types of constraints (i.e. varying size of administrative units, availability of commuting data, potential consistency with already existing core-based metropolitan areas, etc.). The report further displays how open-source computational packages and replicable methods can be used to delineate functional areas in OECD countries based on common guidelines.

A standardised definition of functional areas, as proposed by this report, offers great benefits to policy makers and citizens alike. It can significantly enhance the understanding of rural-urban linkages and local economic development, improve the quality of labour market statistics for small jurisdictions, and facilitate the collaboration of small municipalities outside the areas of influence of cities or large urbanised centres. While some OECD countries have implemented functional areas for their entire national territory in recent years, others lack such expertise. The methodological guidelines developed in this report offer support to those OECD countries with limited experience and expertise in implementing functional areas within their respective national statistical systems and in using functional areas for regional development policies.

Chapter 1. Why delineate functional areas in all territories?

This chapter provides the rationale for delineating functional areas in all territories, not only in urban areas but also in rural areas. It explains how functional geographies can complement administrative geographies. It discusses how functional areas can enrich the collection and computation of territorial statistics. Finally, it illustrates the potential benefits of the concept of functional areas for regional policy.

This chapter outlines the rationale for mapping functional areas in all territories. In OECD countries, the most commonly used type of functional area is based on cities and their economic areas of influence. However, economic linkages that define functional areas exist in all types of territories, urban and rural alike. A comprehensive approach to functional areas, therefore, goes beyond the focus on core-based metropolitan areas, instead aiming to offer the methodology to identify functional areas in all territories and specifically in predominantly rural regions.

To be effective, regional development policy must rely on sound and reliable statistics. A crucial aspect of such statistics is the geographic unit of analysis. In a number of policy domains, administrative boundaries often do not constitute the appropriate geographic scale to fully understand local economies and citizens' economic reality. Instead, the need for meaningful geographies for analysis and policy requires the creation of several concepts, such as metropolitan areas, labour market areas, daily urban systems or, more generally, functional areas. These concepts have been used extensively by OECD countries with the purpose of complementing administrative areas.

While using functional areas can generate benefits in all territories, their predominant existing definitions tend to focus on cities and their surrounding commuting zones. Despite the work carried out and experience gained in a number of countries, the functional organisation of space in predominantly rural areas is something that still needs to be studied in depth from an international comparative perspective. This chapter explains the complementary nature of functional geographies relative to administrative geographies. It then explains how such geography can also offer an enriching perspective with which to look at regional development. Finally, it discusses how it can thus improve policy design and deliver better outcomes for citizens.

Functional and administrative geographies

Traditionally, administrative geographies have been the foundation of territorial statistics. They provide the framework for the production, analysis and understanding of economic and social geography as well as dynamics across space.

Functional areas cannot replace administrative geographies. In fact, they are generally created by clustering small administrative units; hence, functional areas should be regarded and used as an additional, complementary geography that can provide evidence on socio-economic trends across space and can help inform place-based policy. They can enhance the understanding of key economic trends that unfold on a spatial scale that is not properly captured by small administrative geographies. In fact, administrative boundaries sometimes do not adequately capture or reflect the geographic reality of economic activity (Casado Diaz and Coombes, 2011[1]). Furthermore, they can enrich conventional administrative statistics by offering precise information on policy-relevant areas in a way that facilitates better service provision.

A functional approach can improve the effectiveness of public policies. Economic relations, flows of goods and people, do not stop at the administrative border but inherently connect different areas. These economic interdependencies are particularly relevant to topics such as housing, transport and land use, all of which have external effects on neighbouring territories.

In the case of predominantly urban regions, the examples of Paris and Rome succinctly illustrate the challenges that policy makers face when administrative statistics are used to address such policy areas. In both cases, the administrative boundaries of the municipality do not correspond to the actual extent of the city (Figure 1.1). In fact, the administrative boundaries can often differ drastically from the city's reality – or urban area. In Paris, the urban area is much larger than the municipality would indicate. In contrast, the boundaries of the municipality of Rome extend significantly beyond the actual urban area of Rome and includes smaller towns and rural areas. What the two capitals have clearly in common is a discrepancy between their economic or functional reality and the respective administrative areas.

Figure 1.1. Mismatch of municipal boundaries – Paris and Rome

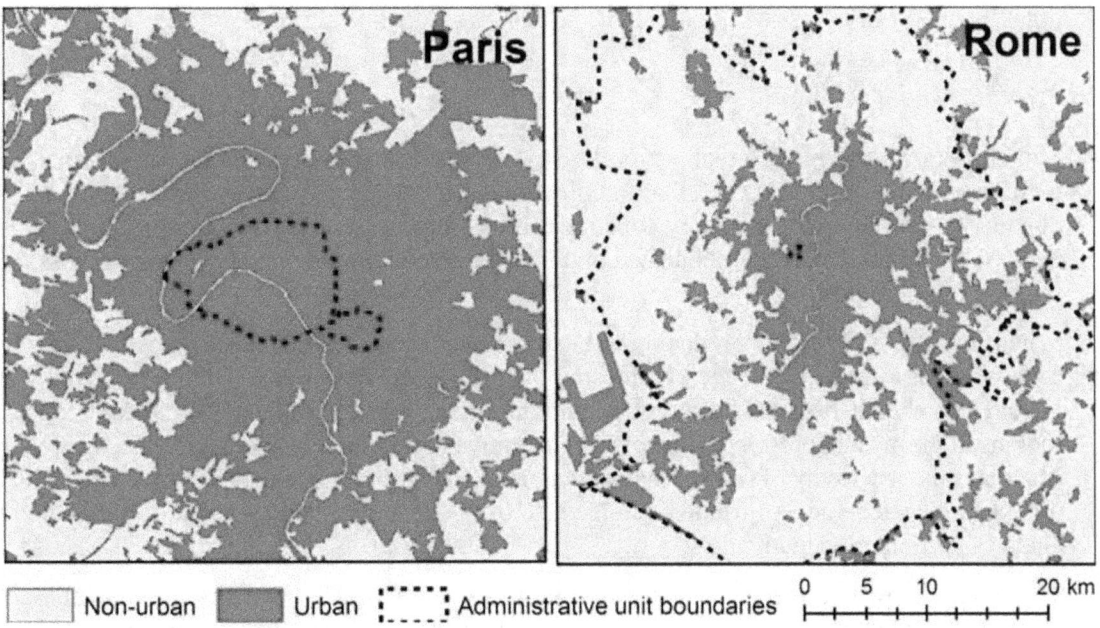

Note: Urban areas in the figure above denote areas with a population density of more than 1 500 inhabitants per square kilometre.
Source: (OECD, 2016[2]).

As Figure 1.1 points out, there is often a scale mismatch between the social or economic reality of the geographies and the way they are structured and defined administratively. This mismatch can have significant implications as using the wrong geographic scale to inform policies can yield ineffective policy choices. National and subnational policy makers need an accurate evidence base on the relevant and respective geographic area to address urgent policy challenges and to ensure effective strategic planning. Administrative boundaries are often, however, the result of historical decisions and circumstances rather than a depiction of the current linkages that could define a region, city or labour market area in a functional sense.

The rise of new sources of data and the increasing availability of different subnational data may likely facilitate the delineation and use of functional areas. In many OECD countries, statistical information on key economic, demographic and social factors is becoming increasingly available at a detailed and more granular subnational level. The geographic granularity often goes beyond large regions (TL2), small regions (TL3) or municipalities. In fact, data are often made available at the level of small statistical enumeration areas or even at a regularly gridded scale.

Functional areas can offer information that is more precise for specific issues and thus enrich statistics that are based on administrative areas. For example, since functional areas are defined according to economic and social territorial linkages, they are likely to offer more meaningful perspective on topics such as employment, economic activity (gross domestic product [GDP] per capita) or earnings (see below for a more detailed discussion). As a consequence, they also allow more tailored policy design and evaluation on issues and challenges concerning those topics and can thus contribute to better living conditions for citizens in a particular place (see below). The rationale for functional areas is not limited to large cities or metropolitan areas. It equally applies to all types of territory as dispersed and complex patterns of mobility and commuting yield territorial linkages outside of large cities.

Better data for all territories: A statistical perspective

Functional areas offer a different perspective on statistics that can produce a more accurate picture of actual circumstances than administrative areas. In particular, socioeconomic conditions are better described by functional rather than administrative areas, precisely because functional areas are delineated and based on economic or social linkages across the territory or region.

When collecting data and producing subnational indicators, national statistical offices (NSOs) often face the challenge of choosing the right geographic scale. On the one hand, having the choice between different geographic areas can enhance policy making by looking at the most appropriate level of administrative areas. On the other hand, this choice illustrates the sensitivity of subnational indicators to changes in the boundaries of territorial units being considered. Adjustments to the size of the area analysed can yield significant changes to subnational indicators.

This issue, known as the modifiable areal unit problem (MAUP) and first prominently discussed by Openshaw, raises the question of whether there is an ideal geographic scale for territorial analysis (Openshaw, 1977[3]; Gehlke and Biehl, 1934[4]). Simply put, the MAUP highlights that the "results of any territorial analysis will partly depend on the areas used for that analysis", meaning that any change to the area considered in the analysis will yield differences in the results (Casado Diaz and Coombes, 2011[1]). The MAUP is particularly pertinent for labour markets and economic indicators. Previous research demonstrates that the choice of subnational areas is relevant for labour market statistics and regional economic indicators such as average GDP per capita, as different scales can lead to significantly different statistics (ESPON, 2007[5]).

Labour market statistics are the primary topic where territorial statistics can benefit from the perspective of functional geographies. Regional economies and therefore regional or local labour markets do not necessarily correspond to administrative units. They are usually significantly smaller than TL2 regions but include various cities and municipalities and can extend beyond as well as across TL3 regions (see Box 1.1 for an explanation of TL2 and TL3 regions). Hence, reporting labour market statistics for established administrative units might yield a better representation of employment, unemployment or labour force participation for a given place than functional geographies would.

> **Box 1.1. OECD territorial classification**
>
> Regions within the 36 OECD member countries are classified by the OECD into 2 territorial levels that reflect the administrative organisation of countries. The 393 OECD large regions (TL2) represent the first administrative tier of subnational government, such as the Ontario Province in Canada. The 2 256 OECD small regions (TL3) correspond to administrative regions, with the exception of Australia, Canada and the United States. These TL3 regions are contained in a TL2 region, with the exception of the United States for which the economic areas cross the states' borders. For Israel and New Zealand, TL2 and TL3 levels are equivalent. For example, the TL2 region of Aquitaine in France encompasses five TL3 regions: Dordogne, Gironde, Landes, Lot-et-Garonne and Pyrénées-Atlantiques.
>
> *Source*: OECD (2019[6]), *OECD Territorial Grids 2019*, OECD, Paris.

In the case of remote or sparsely populated regions, functional areas can constitute a geography that might improve policy makers' understanding of relevant policy challenges. On the one hand, functional areas in rural regions usually bring together (or cluster) administrative units below territorial level 3 (TL3) that are too small in terms of population to generate reliable and representative statistics.[1] On the other hand, in those cases, the higher geographic level of TL3 regions may be too large to represent local labour markets properly. For example, the Canadian version of functional areas, *self-contained labour areas*, illustrates that significant parts of the country's rural and sparsely inhabited administrative units jointly form functional areas with a larger population that might yield the critical mass to allow for reliable subnational indicators for that territory (see Chapter 5 for more details). Thus, clustering together small (below TL3) administrative units may generate an adequate compromise for the proper statistical representation of small territorial units.

Functional areas in the form of local labour markets are necessary for collecting and publishing labour market statistics across countries in a coherent and consistent manner, building on comparable territorial units (Casado Diaz and Coombes, 2011[1]). Taking into account economic territorial linkages ensures that labour market statistics are more informative and give a more representative picture of employment in an economically integrated area. For example, considering a large city and its surrounding suburbs and towns connected by non-negligible commuting flows jointly provide a better representation of labour market statistics than considering each of the municipalities encompassed in the local labour market independently. Similarly, TL2 regions appear not ideal for labour market statistics. Many TL2 regions are large and very heterogeneous in terms of labour force participation and employment. For example, US states such as California or German federal states such as North Rhine-Westphalia can display significantly different internal employment patterns. Thus, they will not capture potentially significant and important geographic disparities in employment or labour force participation.

GDP per capita offers the second illustrative example of how functional areas can enrich existing geographies to provide an accurate description of economic realities through territorial indicators. GDP per capita often serves as an estimate of living conditions or income levels. However, such an approximation can be severely skewed if administrative units are used exclusively to generate subnational indicators on GDP per capita. The economic activity in a place is not necessarily reflective of the GDP or income produced by the residents in that place. For example, in Europe, the GDP per capita in capital cities often significantly overstates income levels of their residents, resulting in between 4% and 76% higher estimated income levels (European Commission, 2007[7]).

The question of the suitability of only using administrative areas for assessing subnational indicators on economic issues highlights the need for a more realistic reflection of the territorial dimension of economic activity and economic linkages. The case of Brussels offers a particularly striking example of the bias of subnational indicators induced by using administrative units as areas of analysis. As a study by ESPON (European Observation Network for Territorial Development and Cohesion) shows, the TL2 Brussels-Capital region is among the wealthiest TL2 regions in Europe in terms of GDP per capita, even though the actual disposable income per inhabitant is even lower than in the two other large Belgian regions, Flanders and Wallonia (OECD, 2019[8]; ESPON, 2006[9]). Sixty percent of workers who contribute to Brussel's GDP do not live in the city but actually commute to work from a different region on a daily basis, which causes income levels in Brussels to appear drastically higher than they are in reality (ESPON, 2006[9]). While income can be generated in a given area, it may still be largely earned and consumed by households in other areas.

Besides greater statistical accuracy for socio-economic indicators, a consistent delineation of functional areas can also help address the challenge of international comparability of subnational statistics. Using the same methodology to identify labour market areas or functional urban areas can yield relatively comparable geographies across different countries. In contrast, administrative boundaries and the size of administrative areas differ vastly across OECD countries. For example, TL2 regions such as federal states in Germany or the US differ substantially in size due to differences in the nature of administrative boundaries. The same is true for TL3 regions across OECD countries.[2] Even more granular data based on municipalities might not be comparable internationally as municipalities in certain countries, e.g. Mexico, tend to be considerably larger than in other countries.[3]

Delineating functional areas also enhances within-country comparability of territorial statistics on socio-economic indicators. For instance, in countries where metropolitan or core-based functional areas are delineated, applying a consistent methodology for functional areas nationally implies that the same approach is used for the whole country and means that the delineation is replicable (Franconi et al., 2017[10]). Ideally, a comprehensive methodology of delineating functional areas should, therefore, generate a partition of the entire country and thus include rural areas or areas remote from major cities.

While functional areas might not be suitable for all statistical purposes, they can complement territorial statistics. No specific unit is ideal for all types of analyses. Instead, the most appropriate geography depends on the purpose of each specific analysis. Functional areas offer an enriching perspective that complements statistics for administrative areas in efforts to accurately capture the spatial dynamics of socio-economic aspects such as employment and GDP per capita.

Better policy design, delivery and evaluation for all territories

In many countries, the focus of functional areas has been placed on urban or (large urban) metropolitan areas. Yet, the concept of functional areas is not exclusive to urban areas but can cover the entire inhabited territory of a country. Economic and social linkages that identify a functionally interlinked area also connect rural areas, villages and towns with each other.

Delineating functional areas for the entire territory is important for fostering social cohesion and economic development across all types of regions and areas by informing the organisation of public service provision and local labour market policy. A set of national functional areas needs to broaden the city-focused perspective to include rural and more remote areas in order to acknowledge their importance for economic growth and development. Understanding the functional connectivity of rural areas enables policy makers to use a targeted and tailored approach to pressing challenges in those areas. For example, problems of public service provision in sparsely populated areas are likely to differ from urban contexts.

Functional areas offer a geography that will likely take into account spatial externalities, as these arise due to economic linkages, which are the defining element of functional areas. Consequently, functional areas can enhance the analysis of policy challenges, the appropriate design of policy action, and the delivery of positive outcomes for residents. Many economic activities create spatial spillovers such as congestion, pollution or effects on housing affordability and availability. These spillovers can cause significant inadvertent negative, but also positive, effects on residents in nearby municipalities, areas or regions. Policies that are based on territorial statistics on administrative units might not appropriately identify these externalities.

The very nature of functional areas implies that they offer a crucial geographic perspective on key subnational policy issues that evolve around territorial linkages. For example, labour market policies can benefit from comprehensive analysis based on information on commuting, which defines people's access to jobs and economic opportunities.[4] Additionally, the economic integration of areas across administrative borders implies that a functional approach to transport planning can help address bottlenecks and identify policy priorities more effectively to alleviate congestion. Furthermore, functional areas reveal information on the geographic patterns of economic opportunities and they can, therefore, be used to examine migration patterns between different labour market areas.

Service provision is another area that can benefit from the information elicited by statistics on functional areas. Commuting flows define a coherent labour market and integrated economic zone, which could also be used as a reference point for assessing access to services. Especially in rural areas that are sparsely populated, providing or maintaining access to public services is increasingly challenging in many OECD countries due to demographic change. To know where and how services in areas with low population density can be best provided, it is essential to understand the functional relationship of neighbouring rural areas because knowing the functional links in non-urban areas yields insights into mobility and transport connectivity in those areas.

Notes

[1] This is based on the internal analyses of the territorial grid used by the OECD, without prejudice to the national statistical conventions of member countries.

[2] As pointed out in Box 1.1, there are a few exceptions, i.e. countries where TL3 regions do not correspond to administrative boundaries.

[3] The issue of contrasts in the way municipal boundaries, and administrative boundaries more generally, are set is also highlighted by Figure 1.1, which compares Paris with Rome.

[4] Please see Casado Diaz and Coombes (2011[1]) for further examples and explanations of the policy relevance of functional areas.

References

Casado Diaz, J. and M. Coombes (2011), "The delineation of 21st century local labour market areas: A critical review and a research agenda", *Boletín de la Asociación de Geógrafos españoles* 57, pp. 7-32. [1]

ESPON (2007), *Preparatory Study on Feasibility of Flows Analysis: Final Report*. [5]

ESPON (2006), *The Modifiable Areal Unit Problem*. [9]

European Commission (2007), *Growing Regions, Growing Europe*, Fourth report on economic and social cohesion. [7]

Franconi, L. et al. (2017), "Guidelines for labour market area delineation process: From definition to dissemination", ISTAT. [10]

Gehlke, C. and K. Biehl (1934), "Certain effects of grouping upon the size of the correlation", *Journal of the American Statistical Association*, Vol. 29/169. [4]

OECD (2019), *OECD Regional Statistics Database*, OECD, Paris. [8]

OECD (2019), *OECD Territorial Grids 2019*, OECD, Paris. [6]

OECD (2016), *Comparison of administrative boundaries and the urban extent of cities*. [2]

Openshaw, S. (1977), "Optimal zoning systems for spatial interaction models", *Environment and Planning*, Vol. A9, pp. 169-184. [3]

Chapter 2. Main approaches and challenges in defining functional areas

This chapter outlines the main approaches used for identifying functional areas in OECD countries. It discusses both core-based as well as multidirectional-flow-based approaches and lays out their most important elements. The chapter also presents key challenges of those approaches in terms of data availability, geographic building blocks, and sensitivity analysis of results.

This chapter discusses and highlights major differences between existing methods to delineate functional areas. It explores approaches to potentially map functional areas in countries where these types of geographies do not yet exist. In so doing, it sets the stage for the mapping exercise presented in this report, for a number of countries where these methods are less frequently used, and discussed in detail in Chapter 5.

The potential benefits of integrating functional areas into the work stream of national statistical offices (NSOs) go beyond the OECD area. An understanding of existing methodological options can help accession countries and non-OECD countries adopt functional area geographies, which will allow them to increase the precision and efficiency of their regional development policies.

To delineate functional areas in all territories, various OECD countries adopt a method based on analysis of multidirectional commuting flows across territorial units, hereafter referred to as a multidirectional-flow-based method. As such, local labour markets are the most commonly used concept for delineating functional areas for a country's entire national territory. They consist of the local area where labour demand and labour supply meet and contain a territory that has significant internal commuting activity but low levels of work-related travel that cross its boundaries.

This chapter mainly focuses on the *prevailing* approach, which: i) identifies clusters according to multidirectional commuting flow intensity instead of urban seeding; ii) builds on using the smallest possible administrative unit; iii) exploits commuting flow data; and iv) extracts information from census sources. However, the methodological implementation can differ across countries in the criteria used in terms of self-containment and population size that a cluster needs to satisfy to yield a functional area.

The following subsections explore some of the major elements that define and can give rise to different approaches for delineating functional areas. The next section discusses the essential distinction between the most common core-based approach and non-core-based approaches for identifying functional areas. Across countries, data sources and geographic building blocks often differ. Furthermore, this chapter also refers to country contexts where commuting flow data between small administrative units are not available and presents some case study examples on how functional areas can nonetheless be identified. The output of different methods depends significantly on the choice of model parameters, which might vary by country, and outcomes can thus be sensitive to that parameter choice, which this chapter discusses. Finally, the chapter concludes with a discussion of further remaining challenges and open questions.

In recent years, some OECD countries have implemented functional areas for their entire national territory. Based on their set of experiences, the concept is now mature enough to deserve a discussion on advantages and disadvantages of existing methods and their data sources as well as on possible recommendations for better comparability across countries (see this chapter and Chapters 3 and 4).

Core-flow-based versus multidirectional-flow-based

Historically, the analysis of functional areas has focused on the metropolitan milieu. In this perspective, linkages between territorial units were generally represented by commuting flows from peripheral, residential areas to core metropolitan areas. This simplification of commuting patterns was also facilitating the computational procedure for the delineation of functional areas, as relatively straightforward rules could be applied to determine the boundaries of such a functional area. The experience of many OECD countries reflects this historical trend, further evidenced by the existing definition of functional urban areas (FUAs) (OECD, 2002[1]).

More recently, data availability and computational capacity on the one hand, combined with a more comprehensive conceptualisation of functional areas on the other hand, have enabled the development of multidirectional-flow-based approach to the delineation of functional areas. A high-level view of these two approaches is represented in Figure 2.1. The core-flow-based approach is usually centred around a city and then includes adjacent areas of economic influence or commuting (this approach is also referred to as *urban seeding*). The multidirectional-flow-based approach considers all mobility flows between different geographic areas to establish their functional relationship. In so doing, it generally provides a more comprehensive representation of linkages between territorial units. While the former approach partitions the territory top down, the latter clusters building block areas bottom up.

Figure 2.1. Core-based and multidirectional-based functional areas

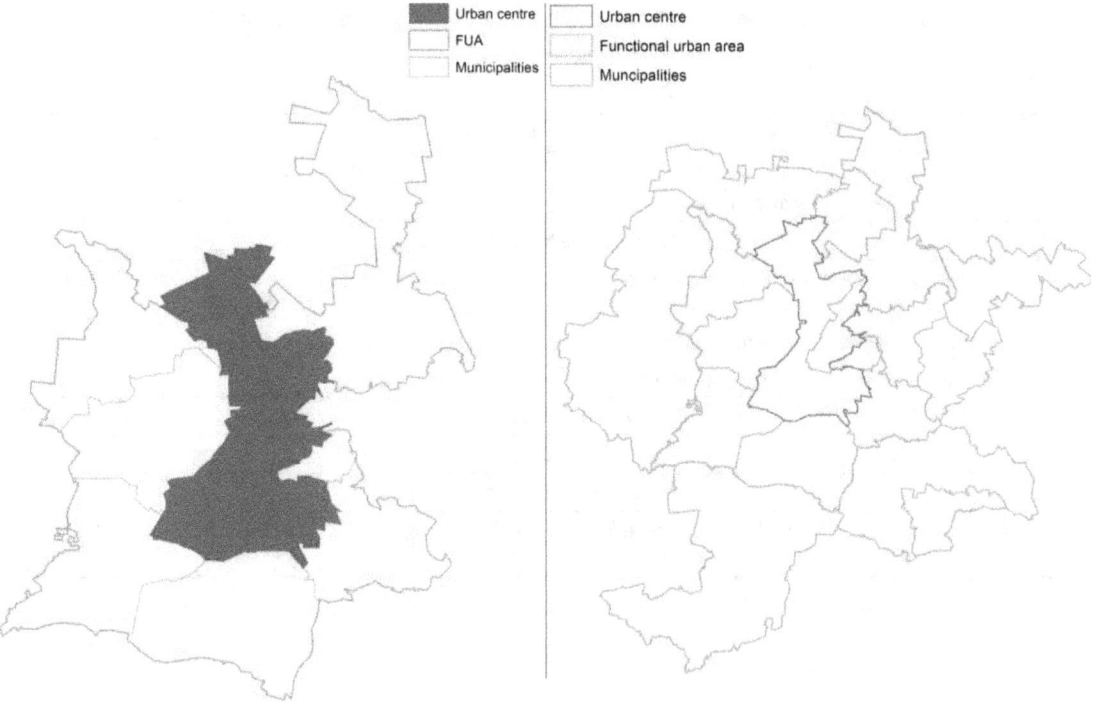

Note: The figure presents the two main approaches to defining functional areas for San Luis Potosí (Mexico). The core-based approach (left) is based on the flow from administrative units (municipalities) to the urban centre (core). The flow-based approach (right) considers the flows between all administrative units.
Source: Produced by the OECD, 2019.

Multidirectional-flow-based approaches are emerging as the prevailing approach in the mapping of functional areas and therefore constitute the focus of this report. However, functional areas defined by multidirectional flows do not substitute core-flow-based areas, such as FUAs. In fact, they represent different concepts that may also serve different purposes. While FUAs consist of nodal commuting flows to a central place, usually a city of a minimum size, and cover a limited territory around those places, functional areas result exclusively from commuting flows between small administrative units and aim to cover the entire territory of a country (Eurostat, 2017[2]).

As discussed in previous work, the distinction between the two approaches can be broken down into a number of key differences (Figure 2.2). First, FUAs are a core-based concept whereas functional areas derive from flow-based analysis.[1] Second, FUAs are limited to the territory surrounding cities while functional areas cover countries' entire territory. Third, the computation of FUAs is less demanding. In comparison, the delineation of functional areas entails a multistep algorithm procedure that requires specific information technology (IT) packages in software such as R or Python. Fourth, the multidirectional flow approach is able to cope with the rapidly growing phenomenon of polycentric urban regions. Finally, small-area-estimation techniques are harder to apply to functional areas due to their geographic configuration and potentially small size.

Figure 2.2. Comparison of core- and multidirectional-flow based approaches

Core flows	Multidirectional flows
Type of interaction	
Nodal type of interaction (commuting is always observed towards a city)	Potentially complex structure of interaction (no central place needed)
Geographical coverage	
Limited to territory around the city	Full coverage of the countries' territories
Method for delineation	
Output geometries in three simple steps; no specialised software needed	Multistep algorithm, IT tool with number of functions is required[2]
Input data needed for delineation	
Commuting flows at the level of small geographic building blocks	Commuting flows at the level of small geographic building blocks
Digital boundaries of local administrative units	Digital boundaries of local administrative units
Granular data on population (i.e. population grid)	
Frequency of the update	
Usually every ten years	
Application of small area estimation (SAE) techniques	
Rather straightforward as the resulting functional areas are an approximation of the metropolitan regions	Rather complex, especially for small functional areas/labour market areas

Source: (Eurostat, 2017[2]).

Geographic building blocks

The underlying geographic building block of subnational data used for the delineation of functional areas is pivotal for functional areas' accuracy. Ideally, the building block should be as granular as possible to provide the highest achievable accuracy of the estimation of functional areas, as long as there are reliable data for such small areas. In general, this means that data should be below the TL3 level. For many countries, such as Korea (see Chapter 5), Mexico or most European Union (EU) countries, data at the municipal level provide the building block for delineating functional areas.

In many cases, building blocks consist of small administrative units such as municipalities, which can, however, vary significantly across OECD countries in terms of geographic extent and population size. The level of detail of building blocks then directly affects the granularity of delineated functional areas. For research purposes, this report explores the delineation of functional areas in a few countries and the respective building blocks of choice for each country will be described (Chapter 5).

Data

The most important source for commuting data is generally national censuses. The information on individuals' place of work and place of residence enables the compilation of aggregate commuting flow patterns between different administrative areas such as municipalities or census tracts. The resulting commuting matrix provides the input data for the algorithm that identifies clusters, i.e. geographic areas with considerable reciprocal mobility patterns.

Commuting patterns are the primary factors in defining and delineating functional areas because they elicit the degree of economic integration between two places as measured by the extent to which workers are willing and able to commute between those two places (Eurostat, 2017[2]).

Additional sources of commuting flow data

A number of alternative data sources to censuses have emerged that can provide useful information for identifying functional areas. The most prominent example is administrative data sources, in particular tax record or employment and business records, in particular national registers of people, business and activities. Several NSOs have developed or are currently developing systems of national registers, which can provide information on the place of residence and the place of work of individuals. In turn, this information can help to estimate mobility flows for any level of geographic aggregation.

Such data can be particularly useful in cases where the collection of commuting data is burdensome and only conducted at irregular intervals. Administrative sources and national registers offer an alternative to census-based commuting flow data that are less cost-intensive and easier to update on a frequent basis.

The emergence of new mobility flow data

In some countries, commuting data are not, or only infrequently, collected through censuses. Furthermore, a number of countries that historically included questions on commuting patterns in their census are currently contemplating a revision of their census that would preclude commuting data. In such contexts, non-traditional data sources and approaches may offer an alternative way of delineating functionally, i.e. economically, integrated areas.

Unconventional data sources such as mobile phone data or credit card data often contain geo-localised information. As a result, mobility patterns of individuals can be detected. Consequently, such data may allow approximations of travel-to-work flows and also provide information on geographic patterns of other economic activity such as consumption.

While commuting data are at the core of the default approaches of delineating functional areas, the availability of mobility flow data is limited in some countries and regions of the world. Usually, national statistics institutes integrate questions on commuting in their national census. Yet, many countries do not collect such information.

Novel approaches building on new sources of data could offer a solution that mitigates a lack of commuting data. Several case study examples indicate how data on mobility derived from mobile phones or credit cards can reveal similar information to commuting surveys:

- Mobility patterns extracted from mobile phone data can yield spatial flow data that help to estimate or approximate work-flow travel. The example of Estonia, discussed in Chapter 5, shows how such data can help to identify territorial linkages between different areas and thus enable the delineation of functional areas.

- Another alternative has emerged through the availability of data on credit card transactions. Exploring the underlying geographic information in financial transaction data can produce spatial patterns of economic activity. Such data even accommodate an additional distinction of functional integration of areas according to the time of the day and year of transactions and thus mobility flows. In a recent study, anonymised records of bank card transactions in Spain helped to develop a new classification of cities with respect to the economic behaviour of their residents (Sobolevsky et al., 2016[3]). Another study uses credit card transaction data to develop a methodology for identifying a cardholder's "usual environment" (Arias et al., 2018[4]).

Approaches without mobility flow data

For specific geographic areas or non-OECD countries in which data availability is very limited, buffer approaches offer yet another alternative to delineating functional areas. Even if commuting data do not exist, road network data are usually available. Hence, drawing a simple zone of, for examples, 10-20 km along the main road network or specific travel times around core urban areas provide a rough approximation of the area of economic influence of an agglomeration. However, such zones do not truly reflect the functional integration of different areas and should thus be seen as second-best option.

Specifications and sensitivity

Delineating functional areas requires country-specific knowledge of, among other things, administrative divisions and commuting patterns. Across countries, administrative units of the same scale can vary in terms of population, area and commuting patterns. The methodology to delineate functional areas captures these differences by allowing users to specify size and self-containment requirements for functional areas.

The size parameters describe the minimum size and target size of a functional area. The self-containment parameter describes the level of self-containment (i.e. people that live and work in the area) required. Generally, the parameters are set so that as the size of the functional area increases the required level of self-containment decreases. In other words, functional areas with a small number of people require a higher share of people living in the area than a larger functional area.

These parameters can be modified to ensure that functional areas provide meaningful agglomerations and are not too large or small for statistical purposes. Chapter 4 provides a technical overview of the process.

The size and self-containment can be also applied when delineating functional areas at different scales within the same country. For instance, commuting data may be available at different levels of geography. More disaggregated scales may yield more precision but may come with more noise. As the geographic units become smaller, there is a higher chance of obtaining isolated functional areas that do not have any linkages. In these cases, it may be useful to aggregate units to reduce the noise in the data and ensure consistent results.

Challenges in analysing and integrating outputs

This section presents and briefly discusses some of the most important challenges in analysing and integrating outputs of methods to delineate functional areas. The subsequent methodological discussion shows prevailing or possible solutions to address these issues. Nonetheless, it should be once again acknowledged that functional areas might not be suitable for all geographic contexts and for all statistical purposes.

The "functionality" challenge

While functional areas can make a valuable contribution to policy making and programme delivery as well as territorial statistics, they might in some cases yield new challenges. For example, clusters identified by commuting flows may, in fact, be impractical from the perspective of service provision or accessibility. In other cases, they might still not reach sufficient critical mass that warrants a dedicated system of public services and infrastructure.

Isolated areas and very small administrative units

Although functional areas ideally offer a meaningful grouping of small administrative units for the entire territory, they might encounter technical difficulties in isolated parts of a country. For example, very small administrative units that are extremely isolated might pose the question of how to integrate and cluster them. This problem can be particularly challenging in large but very sparsely populated regions as is common in Canada but also in parts of Northern Europe. Similar issues arise if information on geographic mobility or commuting patterns is relatively coarse, i.e. only exists for large administrative units that might not fully reveal the exact geographic pattern of commuting between subareas of those administrative units.

Coherence with pre-existing geographic classifications

Any exercise aimed at creating a new geographic concept or even updating and upgrading an existing one faces the challenge of coherence and possible integration with pre-existing concepts and geographic classifications. This challenge is far more compelling when existing geographic concept are deeply entrenched in policy and regulatory frameworks, legislation and delivery of public programmes.

The treatment of pre-existing core-based FUAs is the most salient case, which is made even more sensitive by the similarity between alternative concepts of functional areas (core- versus multidirectional-flow-based). In countries such as Canada and the US, urban core-based functional areas have become an established geography. They are used to disseminate official statistics and also inform policy design and action in domains ranging from housing to transport planning. The pre-existence of such FUAs (or metropolitan areas) constitutes a challenge in finding public acceptance of another potentially overlapping geographic concept.[3]

Therefore, statistical offices face an important choice of including or excluding the administrative areas covered by existing metropolitan areas in their flow-based approach for delineating functional areas. In some countries, the policy and programme relevance of the former might imply that functional areas could only be defined for the remaining national territory and thus offer a complement to metropolitan/functional urban areas. This report presents results for a pragmatic approach to address this type of challenge, which integrates delineated functional areas with pre-existing territorial units, where necessary.

Planning for historical revisions

To remain relevant, functional areas would necessarily be "updated" from time to time or on a regular basis. This requires NSOs to adequately plan for such revisions and take the needed preparatory steps. Contrary to administrative areas, functional areas can evolve, merge or even disappear over time, depending on changing mobility pattern, migration or a shift in economic activity. To capture such changes in territorial linkages, relevant data need to be collected and analysed on a regular basis. In the past, the re-delineation and review of functional areas was a tedious and time-consuming affair. However, open-source programmes with functionality targeted at the specificities of deriving functional or labour market areas are increasingly available. Therefore, any revision of functional areas become less demanding in terms of time and effort.

Notes

[1] The description of functional urban areas (FUAs) apply generally to most types of FUAs, i.e. not only OECD FUAs but also United States metropolitan areas.

[2] Most, but not all, core-based approaches are also multistep and automated and require parametrised functions.

[3] Although the US does not currently have officially recognised functional areas in all territories, the Bureau of Labor Statistics uses their own set of labour market areas (LMAs): https://www.bls.gov/lau/laugeo.htm#geolma. Additionally, the US Bureau of Economic Analysis's *economic areas* present another example of a functional geography beyond metropolitan areas. However, they have neither been updated since 2004 nor used for official statistics since 2013.

References

Arias, J. et al. (2018), "Using transactional data to determine the usual environment of cardholders", in *Information and Communication Technologies in Tourism 2018*, Springer, Cham. [4]

Eurostat (2017), *The Concept of Labour Market Areas – Summary Report*. [2]

OECD (2002), *Redefining Territories: The Functional Regions*, OECD Publishing, Paris, https://dx.doi.org/10.1787/9789264196179-en. [1]

Sobolevsky, S. et al. (2016), "Cities through the Prism of People's Spending Behavior", *Plos One*, Vol. 11/2. [3]

Chapter 3. The current experience of OECD countries

This chapter presents the results of a survey of the OECD Working Party for Territorial Indicators on the existence of predominant concepts of functional areas in OECD countries. The chapter discusses the current experience of OECD countries and gives and overview of the policy relevance of functional areas. Furthermore, the chapter provides more detailed examples and explanations of six cases where functional areas have become a vital tool for statistical and policy purposes.

This chapter reviews the current experience of OECD countries with the application of functional areas for statistical purposes. It presents an overview of applied methods, types of data sources and implementation strategies to identify functional areas in all territories to support policymaking.

The review of existing practices is twofold. First, the results of a survey on the use of functional areas among member countries of the OECD Working Party on Territorial Indicators (WPTI) are assessed. Second, for selected individual OECD countries, existing practices are scrutinised in more detail. Specifically, approaches for delineating functional areas are compared between a North American country (Canada), the pan-European work conducted by Eurostat, as well as four individual European countries (Estonia, France, Italy and the United Kingdom) that use different concepts.

Survey of OECD countries

In a number of OECD countries, functional areas, or similar geographic concepts such as labour market or travel to work areas, are already well established. In spring 2018, the OECD WPTI conducted a survey on existing concepts and policy use of functional areas. Jointly with an earlier cross-national OECD survey in 2002 that examined the relevance of functional delineation of regions on the basis of travel-to-work areas, the WPTI survey highlights the importance of functional areas in OECD member countries (OECD, 2002[1]).

Nine countries reported that a prominent definition or concept of functional areas exists nationally (Figure 3.1). These nine countries also use their respective functional area concept for policy making, either in underlying analysis, the delivery of policies, their monitoring, or their evaluation, showcasing the relevance and potential of functional areas beyond purely statistical aspects. In contrast, one country identifies functional areas solely for a statistical purpose, i.e. not with specific public policies in mind.

A majority of the responding OECD countries use their functional areas to produce and disseminate official statistics. The data on functional areas include indicators on employment statistics, wages, housing demand and supply. Furthermore, indicators also cover demographic topics such as migration patterns and population dynamics. Finally, various countries also provide mobility and commuting flow data for their respective national functional areas. These indicators provide not only the necessary information for policy design and evaluation in a range of policy areas (see the following section for more detail) but also feed into academic research.

In light of the increasing importance of functional areas, Eurostat initiated in 2013 the *Task Force on Harmonised Labour Market Areas* to make an official proposal of the European Commission's position on the subject. The group included representatives of national statistical offices (NSOs) from France, Hungary, Italy, the Netherlands, Poland and the United Kingdom, all of which are OECD member countries. The task force exchanged research as well as existing approaches and new ideas on delineating labour market areas in European Union (EU) countries. It developed a harmonised methodology based on standardised definitions, replicable in all EU countries and presented the final report to the Eurostat Working Group on regional, urban and rural development statistics. Eurostat then launched a grant to produce harmonised national labour market area (LMA) geographies according to the European methodology.[1]

Figure 3.1. WPTI survey on the use of functional areas

Question	Yes	No	No response	Partly
Is there a prominent definition or concept?	9	2		
Is it used in policy? (e.g. delivery, analysis, monitoring, evaluation)	9		1	1
Is it used for/in statistical dissemination?	7	2		2

Note: Responses as given by WPTI delegates. Apart from Eurostat, the following members participated: Denmark, France, Germany, Italy, Mexico, the Netherlands, Poland, Spain, Switzerland, the United Kingdom and the United States. No responses were received from the remaining OECD member countries.
Source: OECD Working Party on Territorial Indicators (OECD, 2018[2]).

The grant was the occasion to support the further development of LMAs in Europe in a number of ways. First, Istat developed an information technology (IT) tool, the R package LabourMarketAreas, containing modules to deal with any stage of the LMAs delineation process, from algorithm implementation to fine-tuning, visualisation, analysis and dissemination (see Franconi et al. (2017b). Furthermore, as part of the grant, documentation and training material related to the computation of LMAs, including specific training on the software package R organised by Istat, were published. Finally, the *Guidelines for Labour Market Area Delineation Process: From Definition to Dissemination*[2] were shared among the participants and released. In 2018, Eurostat promoted a task force on *Establishment of a European set of labour market areas* which aims to be a platform for exchange and reflection regarding possible future refinements but also future challenges to functional areas, i.e. the regular availability of commuting flows data. The task force develops typologies for characterising LMAs and methods to further harmonise and make LMAs comparable across Europe.

Examples of policy application in OECD countries

Functional areas, including functional urban areas (FUAs), have found wide use in policy design, analysis and policy evaluation in OECD countries. Below is a selected but not exhaustive list of topics that demonstrates the variety of subjects that can benefit from functional areas:

- **Employment policies:** The most prominent policy domain for which functional areas have been used. In France, the "Macron law" proposes to utilise functional areas as units of analysis for employment policies such as reinforcing competition is certain professions. Germany uses information on several indicators such as unemployment rate and wage rates for its 258 labour market areas to allocate resources from a joint federal/state aid programme for lagging regions.

- **Industrial development:** In the United Kingdom (UK), functional areas have been used to target funding for industrial development.
- **Industrial renewal policy:** Italy uses labour market areas to first identify territories of industrial crisis and then monitor the effect of revamping policies.
- **Public transport planning:** Several countries such as Estonia use data on daily traffic flows in their national labour market areas to improve public transport provision.
- **Housing needs:** In the UK, housing market areas have been used to assess housing needs in the country by identifying and comparing local housing supply and demand.
- **Market rents/rent control:** The United States uses the geographies of metropolitan areas to assess income limits for rental subsidy programme eligibility. Additionally, metropolitan and micropolitan areas are used to establish maximum loan amounts for federally insured mortgages.[3]
- **Land use:** Travel to work areas in Denmark have proven useful for the analysis of land use and have featured in various publications on that topic.
- **Cross-border commuting:** The high level of foreign workers who commute to work in Luxembourg has led to efforts in identifying and analysing cross-border flows and commuting patterns between Belgium, France, Germany and Luxembourg. Similarly, Switzerland has produced cross-border labour market areas to account for the large flows of workers travelling across borders every day.
- **Local government collaboration and restructuring:** In order to have a better fit of municipalities with the functional reality of territorial economic linkages, Finland has taken into account the boundaries of its labour market areas.

The list above demonstrates the manifold and diverse possibilities to make use of functional areas in analysis and policy making. The concept of functional areas can help design, monitor and scale programmes and policies at the right geographic level.

Detailed country examples of functional areas

The following subsections describe different existing sets of functional areas in several OECD countries in more detail. The list includes both countries that have functional areas covering the entire national territory (typically with a multidirectional-flow-based approach) and countries that delineate functional areas only for a subset of their territory (typically with a core-flow-based approach). The example of Estonia provides an alternative approach, illustrating how novel sources of data can replace or refine traditional sources of data in identifying territorial linkages.

Several European countries have been working together on the labour market areas (LMAs) concept of functional areas. The collaboration began in 2013/14 with the Task Force on Harmonisation, which aimed to support the switch from national concepts to a common, harmonised EU method. The work was continued with the 2016/17 grant exercise, which focused on efforts to produce national and cross-border LMAs based on a common IT tool. A new task force was initiated in 2018 to establish a European dataset of labour market areas.[4]

Countries participating in these various activities with the aim of developing a harmonised geography are Bulgaria, Denmark, Finland, France, Germany, Hungary, Italy, the Netherlands, Poland, Portugal, Switzerland and the United Kingdom. It has not been used so far at EU level but several Directorate Generals (DGs) of the European Commission (e.g. Regional and Urban Policy, Employment, and Transport) have expressed interest in utilising LMAs for their work. So far, labour market areas have only found application in analytical publications at the European level. The task force strives to harmonise the concept of labour market areas in Europe to reach its full potential for EU policy making (Eurostat, 2017[3]).

The Eurostat task force computed functional areas for a number of participating countries. The delineation of functional areas in those countries followed an experimental approach agreed upon in the task force. Annex A presents the examples of four participating countries: Bulgaria, Finland, Hungary and Portugal.

The comparability issue is of extreme importance in an international setting. In Europe, harmonisation and comparability are crucial. In the initial task force, a first step has been made with the creation of a common European method. However, it is evident that different countries adopt different parameters because they have different aims, different commuting structures and different distributions in the territories. Therefore, further steps need to be taken to improve comparability. Harmonisation was the key topic of the final workshop of the grant.[5] Several ideas came out; in particular, Thomas Thorsen from Statistics Denmark[6] suggested two approaches: method and output-oriented harmonisation.

The 2018 task force studies the "method-oriented harmonisation" approach: national (local) LMAs are aggregated to reach European (regional) LMAs. The idea is that the aggregation process made by means of the same R package *LabourMarketAreas* and common European parameters will lead to comparable functional regions.

Another perspective, the "output-oriented harmonisation", is based on the definition of common criteria that output should meet. Examples of such criteria could be:

- All EU LMAs should be more than 50% self-contained – supply side as well as demand side.
- At least 70% of employed persons should live in EU LMAs that are at least 70% self-contained supply side – and similarly for demand side.

Canada

Statistics Canada has developed two types of functional areas. The first, census metropolitan areas (CMA) and census agglomerations (CA), consist of the area of one or more adjacent municipalities (census subdivisions, CSDs) centred around a population centre (known as the core) (Statistics Canada, 2012[4]). While a CMA needs to have a total population of at least 100 000 of which 50 000 or more must live in the core, a CA must have a core population of at least 10 000 but has no other total population requirement. Municipalities belong to a CMA or CA if they are highly integrated with the core, as measured by commuting flows. CMA and CA delineation methodology imposes a higher commuting requirement than the current OECD functional urban areas (FUAs). A municipality belongs to a CMA or CA if at least 50% of the labour force living in a municipality work in the core of the CMA/CA.

In addition to core-based functional areas, Statistics Canada has also experimented with a functional area geography called self-contained labour areas (SLAs). Compared to

CMAs/CAs, SLAs offer much larger geographic coverage. They define all municipalities using commuting data in Canada. Each area consisting of one or several CSDs where the majority of residents both work and live constitute a self-contained grouping of areas (Alasia, 2016[5]). Self-containment has two aspects: i) self-containment of workers (percentage of area jobs that are filled by area residents); and ii) self-containment of residents (percentage of area residents who have jobs in the area). The minimum threshold for self-containment is 75%.

The concepts of CMAs and CAs have found wide use in policy and programme delivery. In contrast, SLAs only contribute to policymaking in some Canadian provinces. Statistically, CMAs and CAs are well established within the national statistical system and a multitude of statistical indicators is available at that scale. For SLAs, some federal departments have started requesting tabulation of labour market indicators using this geography.

United Kingdom

Functional areas have a long tradition in the UK. Travel to work areas (TTWAs) were first delineated and became the official British labour market areas in the 1960s. Today, there are 228 travel to work areas in the UK based on 2011 Census data, of which 149 are in England, 45 in Scotland, 18 in Wales, 10 in Northern Ireland and 6 extend across borders (Figure 3.2).[7]

TTWAs intend to approximate LMAs. They aim to reflect self-contained areas, i.e. areas in which most people both live and work. Currently, 75% of an area's resident workforce needs to work in the area and at least 75% of the people who work in the area must also live in the area in order for that area to be self-contained. Furthermore, the economically active population of the area needs to be at least 3 500. In areas with a working population of more than 25 000, the self-containment criterion is only 66.7%, thereby allowing a trade-off between workforce size and level of self-containment.

Coombes (2015[6]) identified the 2011 TTWAs through a matrix of commuting flow data by origin and destination for workers aged 16 and over, based on residence postcode and address of the main job's workplace, all derived from the 2011 Census. The following statistical geographies are the building blocks for TTWAs in 2011: lower layer super output areas (LSOAs) in England and Wales, data zones (DZs) in Scotland, and super output areas (SOAs) in Northern Ireland.

The Office of National Statistics (ONS) provides a rich set of statistical information on the full set of the 2011 version of TTWAs in the UK. Apart from population data, territorial statistics of TTWAs also cover labour market participation (employment and participation rates, full- and part-time employment and self-employment), social benefits data, educational attainment and other relevant demographic, socioeconomic information such as gender or age, and information on the respective method of travel to work.[8]

Figure 3.2. Functional areas in the UK: 2011 travel to work areas (TTWAs)

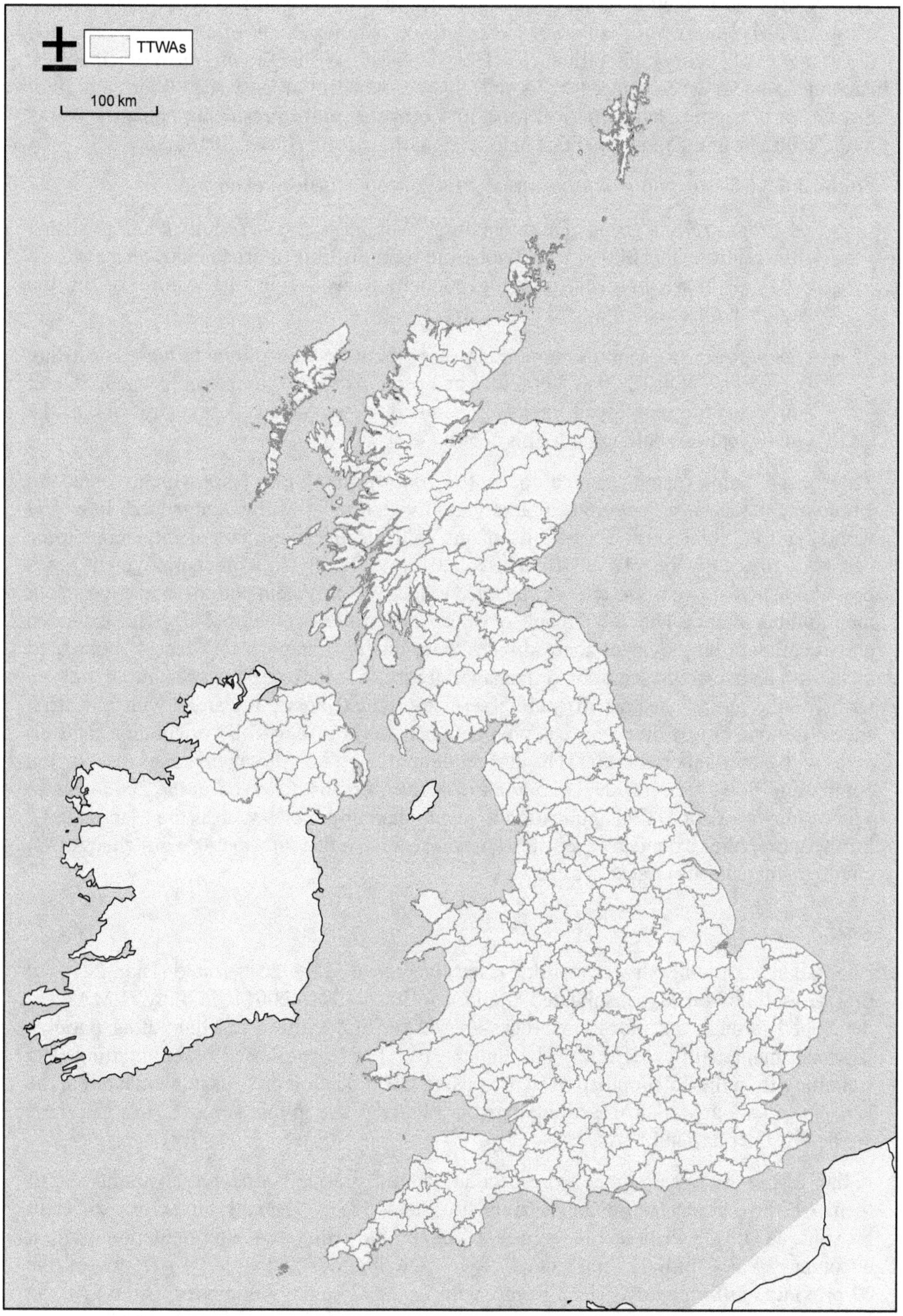

Source: Authors elaboration on travel to work area boundaries (ONS, 2019[7]).

France

The INSEE, the French national statistical office, has developed two types of functional areas. *Aires urbaines* or urban areas identify the economic extent of cities, i.e. cities and their areas of economic influence. They consist of neighbouring municipalities, encompassing an urban centre (urban unit) that accounts for at least 10 000 jobs and rural districts or urban periphery where at least 40% of the employed resident population works in the centre or in the municipalities belonging to this centre (Insee, 2016[8]).

Following the 2010 zoning of urban areas, this concept has been extended:

- *Average areas*: a group of municipalities, without pockets of empty land, consisting of a centre with 5 000 to 10 000 jobs and rural districts or urban units where at least 40% of the employed resident population works in the centre or in the municipalities belonging to this centre.

- *Small areas*: a group of municipalities, without pockets of empty land, consisting of a centre with 1 500 to 5 000 jobs and rural districts or urban units where at least 40% of the employed resident population works in the centre or in the municipalities belonging to this centre.

The second major functional area concept is *zones d'emploi or* employment zones. An employment zone is a geographical area within which most of the labour force lives and works, and in which business establishments can find the main part of the labour force necessary to occupy the jobs on offer (Insee, 2016[9]). The division into employment zones provides a breakdown of the territory adapted to local employment patterns and covers both metropolitan France and the French overseas departments (Figure 3.3). The extended classification of employment zones divides them into six categories: i) densely populated areas with an over-representation of managerial jobs; ii) relatively low specialised areas in terms of the tertiary sector; iii) public service-oriented areas; iv) areas with industrial specialisation; v) low-density areas with an agricultural or agri-food orientation; and vi) areas with a tourism orientation. The current delineation of employment zones rests on the commuting flows from residence to work of active persons observed in the 2006 census. The employment zones find application in several labour policies such as the Macron law.[9] Furthermore, the extended classification presents useful information on changes in employment patterns or access to services.

Italy

The Italian National Statistics Institute (Istat) has released the 2011 round (Istat, 2014[10]) of LMAs following a consolidated tradition (1981, 1991, 2001). In Italy, LMAs are developed through an allocation process based on the analysis of commuting patterns between municipalities (LAU2). The Italian 2011 LMAs are based on commuting data stemming from the 15th Population Census using the allocation process implemented in the R package LabourMarketAreas, illustrated in Figure A.C.1 in the Annex C. In total, there are 611 distinct Italian LMAs.

Italian LMAs are not designed to respect any administrative boundary constraints: 56 of them (9.2%) cut across regional boundaries and 185 (30.3%) span across different provinces (TL3). Milan is the biggest LMA in Italy in terms of population size: it encompasses 3.7 million inhabitants, 174 municipalities belonging to 7 out of the 12 provinces in Lombardy (TL2). Rome, with its 3 892 square kilometres, is the LMA in Italy with the largest territory, the smallest being Capri (10.5 square kilometres).[10]

Figure 3.3. Functional areas in France

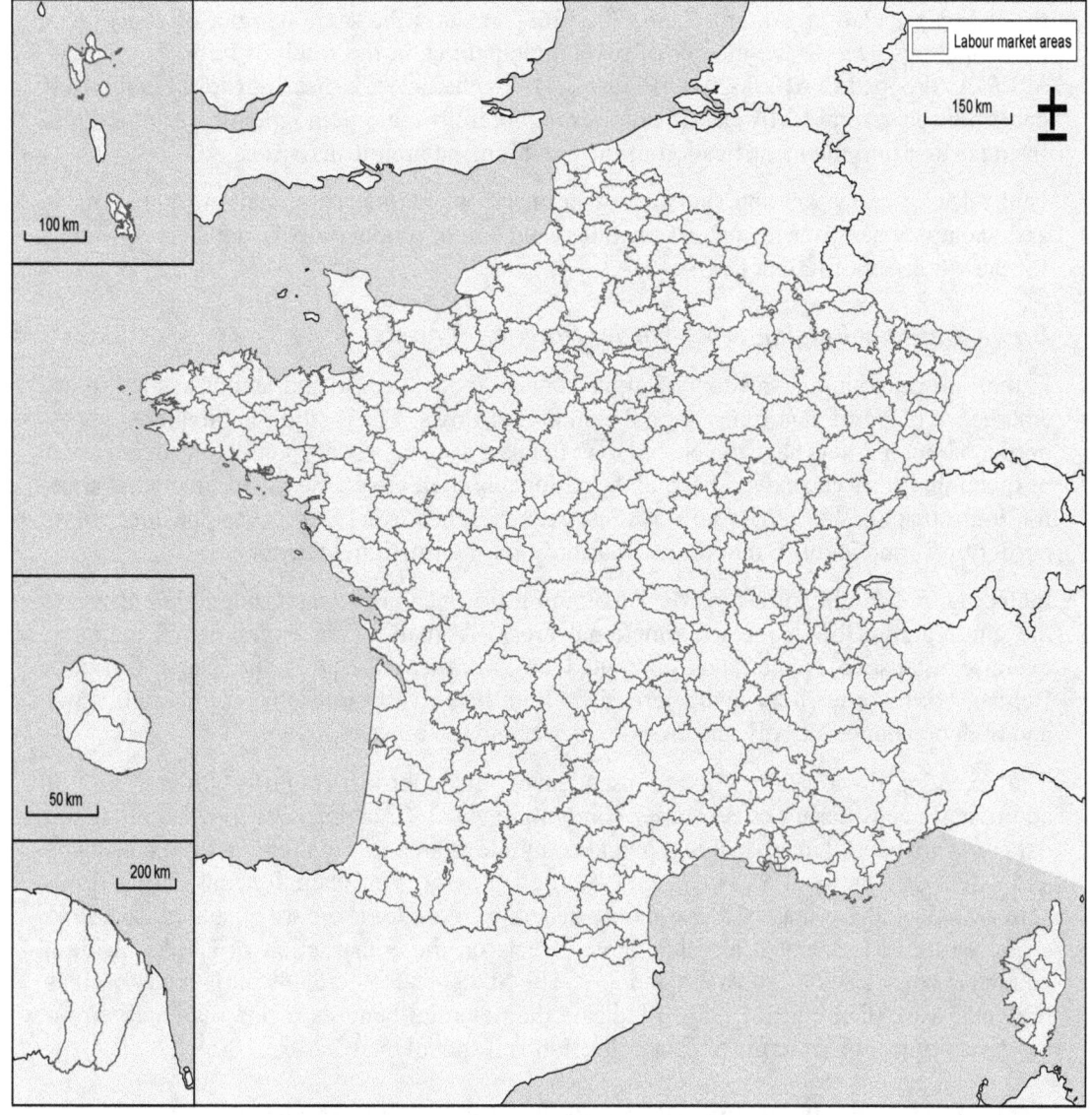

Note: The figure presents French labour market areas.
Sources: Observatoire des territoires (2019); INSEE; Institut d'aménagement et urbanisme de la région Ile-de-France (IAU-IdF).

In order to qualify as an LMA, the local, economically active population of an area needs to be of at least 1 000. In areas with a working population of more than 10 000, the self-containment criterion is only 60%, again acknowledging the potential trade-off between workforce size and level of self-containment.

Nearly half of Italian LMAs (279) fall into the 10-50 000 inhabitant size class, whereas the highest proportion of the population (35.0%) lives in LMAs with 100 000 to 500 000 inhabitants. In 332 LMAs (combing over 70% of the national population), more than three-quarters of the labour force lives and works in the same LMA (self-containment is more than 75%).

The 2011 LMAs show a high level of consistency with the previous 2001 edition: 556 current LMA also exist in the previous list of LMAs (91.0%) and represent 96.6% of the Italian population. Among them, 201 (36.7%) show the same number of constituent municipalities. Due to the merger of two municipalities in the south of Italy, the number of LMAs dropped to 610 in 2018 (Figure 3.4). To characterise these territorial units, Istat has produced several LMA classifications ranging from socio-demographic to cultural and from territorial to the identification of the prevailing economic activities.

Istat releases indicators and statistical data on labour market participation (employment and unemployment rate from 2006 onwards) and labour productivity (from 2015 onwards) for the whole set of Italian LMAs.[11]

Dutch-German-Belgian cross-border functional areas

In the European Union, freedom of movement of goods, people and labour has led to the emergence of significant transnational commuting flows. Thus, multiple integrated cross-border labour markets have developed over the past decades. Conceptually, the delineation of functional areas can extend beyond the national border. Given the use of functional areas for domestic policy or territorial statistics, countries, however, tend not to consider cross-border flows and identify functional areas only for their national territory.

Including or excluding cross-border commuting flows can have a considerable impact on the configuration of delineated functional areas. As part of an experimental mapping exercise, Statistics Netherlands computed cross-border LMAs at the Dutch-German-Belgian border, a territory characterised by both historically intensive commuting flows and high population density and cross-border economic clusters.

The exercise demonstrated the consequences of ignoring country borders, i.e. of additionally considering cross-border commuting flows (Eurostat, 2017[3]). By including data on employees that are resident in and commute from a foreign region, the exact shape and extent of functional areas changed along the border. For example, considering flows across the Dutch-German border not only generates more logical clusters and gives rise to cross-border LMAs, but it also has large effects on the construction of LMAs inside a country's boundaries (Figures 3.5 and 3.6). The Statistics Netherlands initiative as well as previous work (Coombes, 1995[11]) indicate the potential benefits of international, cross-border co-operation in terms of data collection and spatial analysis.

Estonia: Mobile positioning data for delineation of functional areas

Estonia offers an illustrative example of the possibilities that new or unconventional sources of data might yield for both identifying functional, territorial linkages and producing territorial statistics for those areas. In Estonia, functional areas have been delineated by mobile positioning data in two studies commissioned by the Ministry of the Interior and conducted by the Mobility Lab of the University of Tartu (Ahas and Silm, 2013[12]; Ahas et al., 2010[13]). These studies have served as an input to administrative reform, such as the Estonian Regional Development Strategy 2014-2020, the National Spatial Plan of Estonia 2030 and several other county spatial plans.

Figure 3.4. Italian LMAs

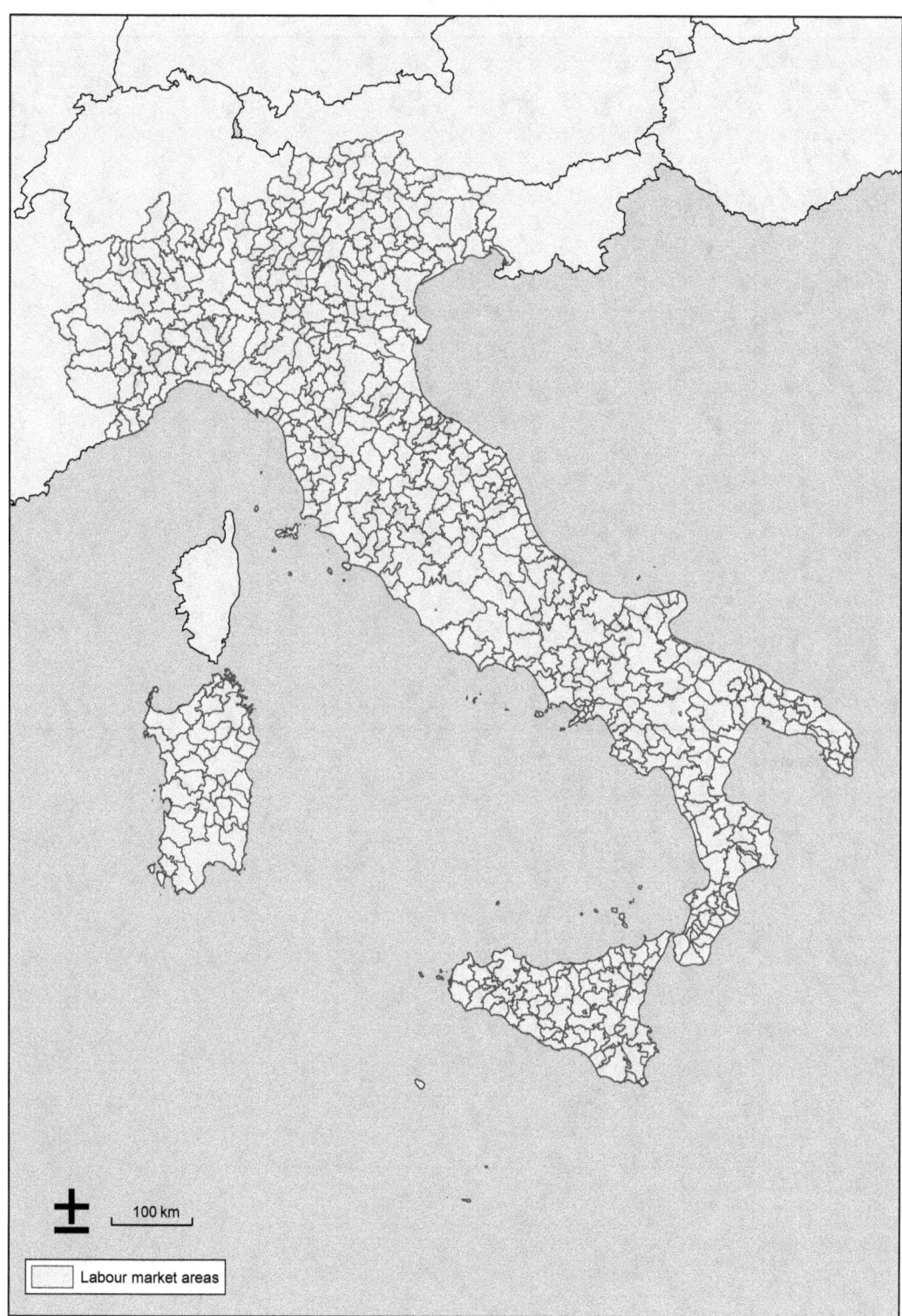

Source: Authors elaboration on labour market areas provided by Istat (2019).

Figure 3.5. LMAs without cross-border information: Belgium, the Netherlands and North Rhine-Westphalia

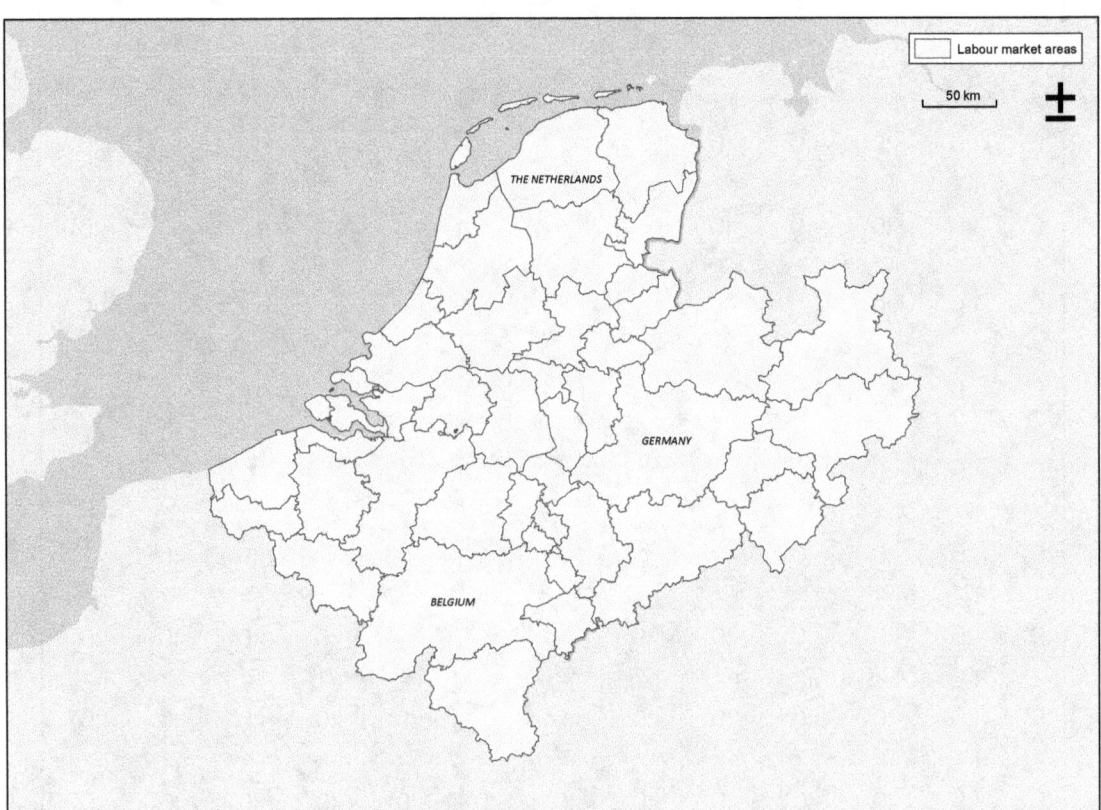

Source: Shapefiles provided by Statistics Netherlands.

Figure 3.6. LMAs with cross-border information: Belgium, the Netherlands and North Rhine-Westphalia

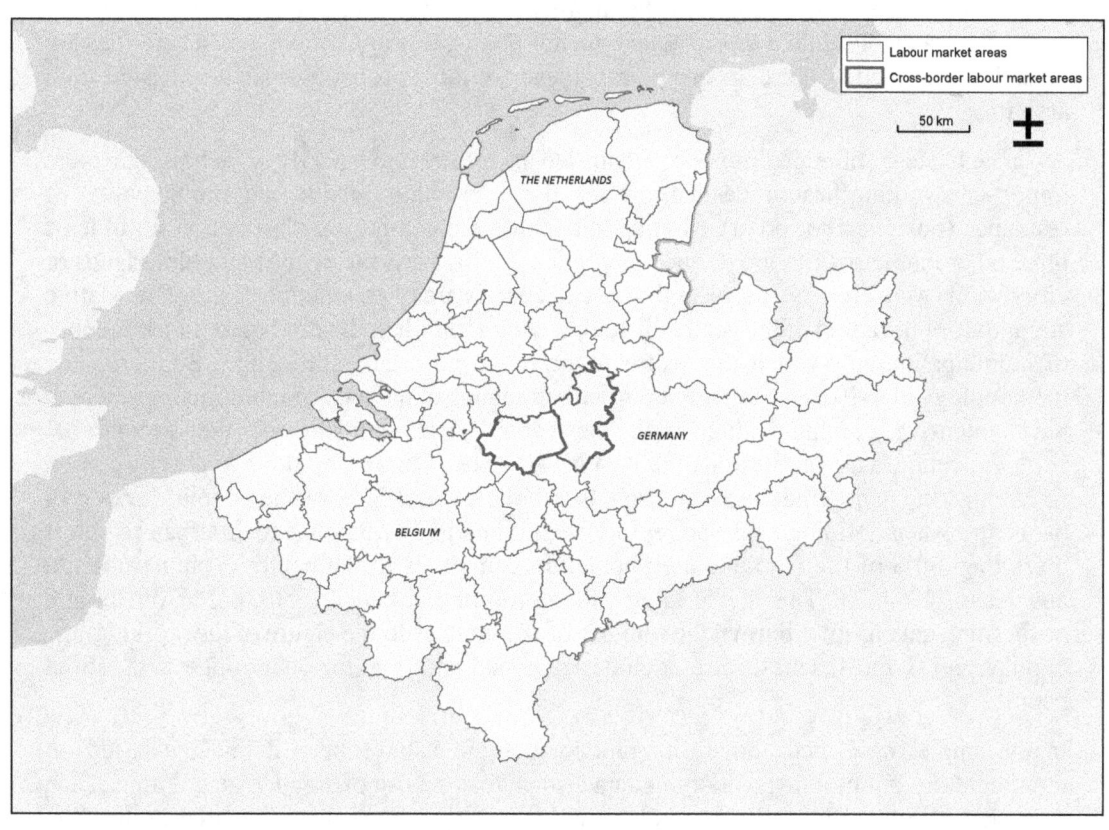

Source: Shapefiles provided by Statistics Netherlands.

The methodology for the delineation of functional areas is based on passive mobile positioning data. These data are automatically stored in the memory files of mobile network operators. The Estonian case studies used the most common form of passive mobile positioning data, which are call detail records (CDR). A CDR database contains all call activities initiated by a mobile phone user: incoming and outgoing calls and sent messages (SMS, MMS). Call activities are recorded in the host mobile network, while these are received via the roaming service when abroad. The data contain the following variables: i) a unique identification code for each phone user (usually randomly generated by the mobile network operator to anonymise the database for researchers); ii) the start time of the call activity; and iii) the geographical co-ordinates of the network antenna that provided the network signal for the call activity. The spatial accuracy of passive mobile positioning depends on the geographical division of the mobile network, which is not equally distributed in space. Call activities are initially registered within one second.

Locations of call activities have been considered as a proxy for human presence. Home, work-time location and secondary anchor points for each individual can be identified based on call activities. Anchor points are determined using a special model based on the location and the timing of the call activities of each user over a period of one month (Ahas et al., 2010[14]). The Estonian studies have shown that the locations of the call activities recorded during the course of a long observation period (at least one calendar month) could be used to describe the activity space and important anchor points (residence, work) of an individual rather well (Silm and Ahas, 2010[15]; Ahas et al., 2010[14]). The movements between individuals' anchor points are aggregated to identify home-work and home-secondary anchors commuting flows. Only the most important secondary anchor point of each individual is taken into account in the aggregation, as there could be several secondary anchors for an individual. For secondary anchor points, it is not known which activities are actually performed at these anchor points; these are most probably related to leisure time activities.

As a next step, municipalities are identified as centres to specify which is the most important working/leisure destination for those moving outside the municipality of residence (home anchor point). Municipalities that are commuting destination for at least three other municipalities are defined as centres. In this way, the centres and hinterlands or city regions were created. It is clear that not all centres are of equal importance. The relative strength (or relevance) of the centres is found using a simple indicator based on the number of municipalities for which the centre is the most important destination. Similarly, the methodology identifies urban regions. An urban region is made up of municipalities, which have intensive communication with the centre. The indicator of the strength of communication is the proportion of the working-age residents commuting to the city centre. In Estonia, the main guideline is to use a threshold level of 30% of the people working in the centre when defining an urban region, i.e. a municipality belongs to an urban region if more than 30% of the working-age population commutes to the centre (Tammaru, Kulu and Kask, 2004[16]). The methodology for delimiting urban regions based on mobile positioning data has not limited the number of commuters to the centre to the working-age population, as the database also includes daily commuting for school-age and retired people.

In the studies described above, the functional regions have been delineated based on municipalities but mobile positioning data also enable the use of smaller spatial units, such as territorial communities (https://mobilitylab.ut.ee/OD/). Equally, in the cited studies, the functional areas have been found to be based on movements within Estonia, but mobile positioning data also allow to estimate flows for cross-border movements based on mobile network operators roaming data. Each mobile network operator can provide data related to its own country (domestic, inbound and outbound) so that movements and directions related to a country can be elicited. For example, the data reveal where people go from Estonia and from where people come to Estonia. If similar data were available for all countries, the same methodology could be used for finding cross-border movements and functional regions. In addition, if there are also social characteristics of the people (for example gender, age, nationality, etc.) taken into account, the commuting flows could be found for different social groups. Functional regions for different types of movers (for example tourists, regular movers, students, etc.) could be identified the same way. Besides physical movements, the mobile positioning data allow delineating the functional areas based on social networks, for example flows between callers' and calling partners' places of residence.

The more mobile network operators' data are included in a structured database, the more comprehensive the dataset becomes. In these studies, data from one mobile network operator were used. The main limitation of using passive mobile positioning data is access to the data because mobile network operators are hesitant to provide it. There is a relatively long value chain of implementing mobile positioning data, which requires expertise from several research fields simultaneously (Ahas et al., 2008[17]). Besides ethical issues and privacy concerns, lack of ground truth data to validate obtained mobility findings have hindered the implementation of the method so far.

Figure 3.7. City centres, urban areas and their economic area of influence in Estonia

Estimated functional relationships based on mobile phone data

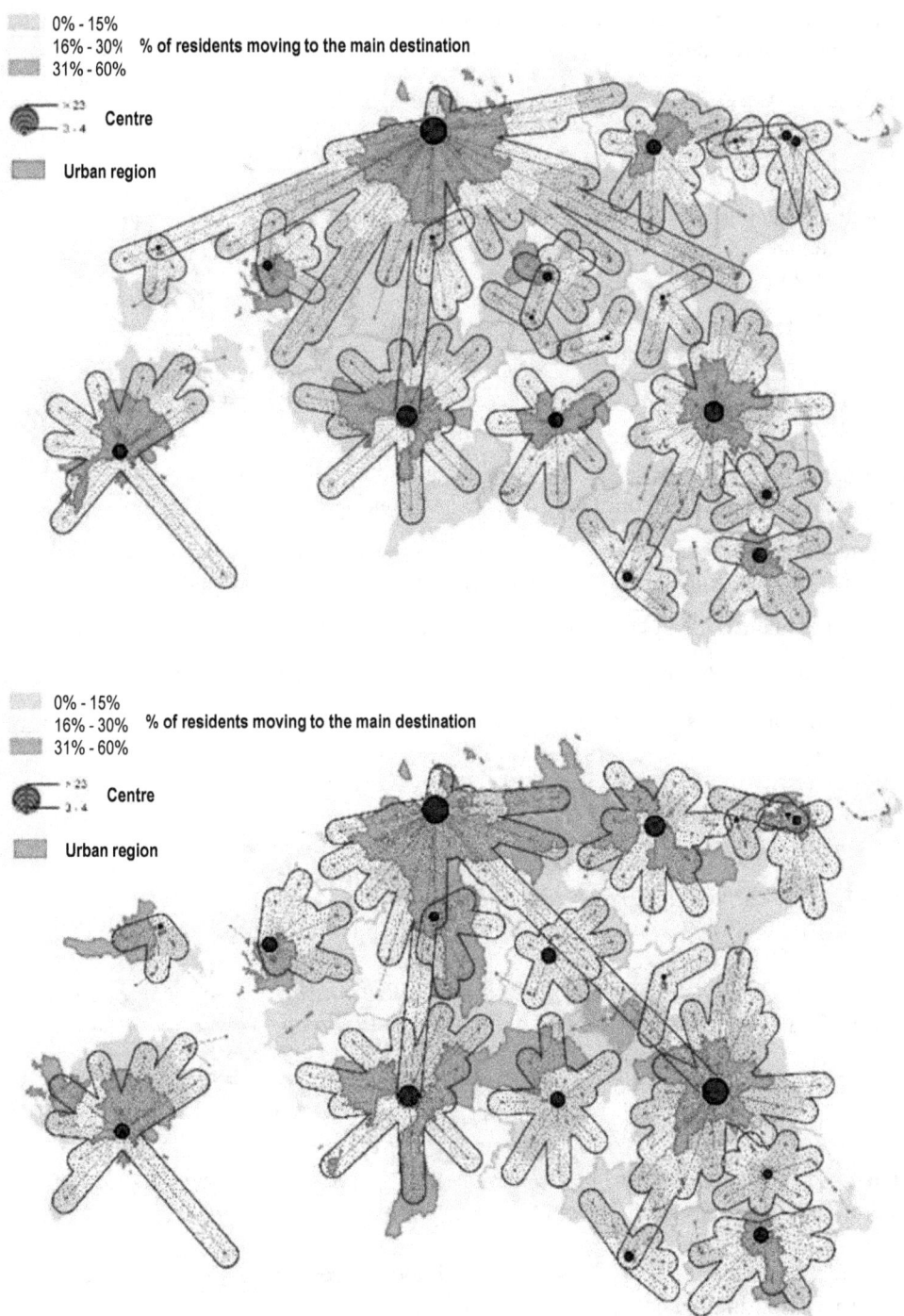

Note: Centres, urban regions and hinterlands found by home and work-time anchor points (top panel) and by home and secondary anchor points (bottom panel).
Source: Ahas, R. et al. (2010[13]), *Regionaalne pendelrändeuuring (Regional Commuting Study)*, Report, Chair of Human Geography and Regional Planning, University of Tartu.

Notes

[1] Functional areas in all territories correspond to local labour markets. In EU countries, the predominant term for this geography is LMA. For EU countries, the terms functional areas and LMAs are used interchangeably.

[2] https://ec.europa.eu/eurostat/cros/system/files/guidelines_for_lmas_production08082017_rev300817.pdf.

[3] https://www.hud.gov/program_offices/housing/fhahistory.

[4] Eurostat has established a dedicated web portal for the work and discussion of the task force on labour market areas in the EU: https://ec.europa.eu/eurostat/cros/content/labour-market-areas_en (Eurostat, 2019[18]).

[5] Slides available at: https://ec.europa.eu/eurostat/cros/content/labour-market-areas-current-development-and-future-use-rome-16-june-2017_en.

[6] Available at: https://ec.europa.eu/eurostat/cros/content/optimizing-parameters-%E2%80%93-or-maybe-not_en.

[7] Mike Coombes from the University of Newcastle led the work producing the 2011 TTWAs in the UK, following earlier work outlined in (Coombes and Bond, 2008[19]).

[8] For more detailed information see: https://www.ons.gov.uk/employmentandlabourmarket/peopleinwork/employmentandemployeetypes/articles/traveltoworkareaanalysisingreatbritain/2016.

[9] The full name of the law is "Loi pour la croissance, l'activité et l'égalité des chances économiques".

[10] Shape files are available at: http://www.istat.it/storage/sll2011/SLL2011_shapefile.zip.

[11] More information exists under the following link: https://www.istat.it/en/labour-market-areas.

References

Ahas, R. et al. (2008), "Evaluating passive mobile positioning data for tourism surveys: An Estonian case study", *Tourism Management*, Vol. 29/3, pp. 469-486. [17]

Ahas, R. and S. Silm (2013), *Regionaalse pendelrände kordusuuring (Re-study of Regional Commuting)*, Chair of Human Geography and Regional Planning, University of Tartu. [12]

Ahas, R. et al. (2010), "Using mobile positioning data to model locations meaningful to users of mobile phones", *Journal of Urban Technology*, Vol. 17/1, pp. 3-27. [14]

Ahas, R. et al. (2010), *Regionaalne pendelrändeuuring (Regional Commuting Study)*, Report, Chair of Human Geography and Regional Planning, University of Tartu. [13]

Alasia, A. (2016), "Operationalizing 'Self-contained Labour Areas' as a potential standard geography for disseminating Statistics Canada data". [5]

Coombes, M. (1995), "The impact of international boundaries on labour market area definitions in Europe", *Area*, Vol. 27/1, pp. 46-52. [11]

Coombes, M. and S. Bond (2008), "Travel-to-Work Areas: the 2007 review", *Office for National Statistics, London.* [19]

Coombes, M. and ONS (2015), *Travel to Work Areas*, https://www.ncl.ac.uk/media/wwwnclacuk/curds/files/RR2015-05.pdf. [6]

Eurostat (2019), *https://ec.europa.eu/eurostat/cros/content/labour-market-areas_en*. [18]

Eurostat (2017), *The Concept of Labour Market Areas – Summary Report.* [3]

Insee (2016), *Employment Zone*, Institut national de la statistique et des études économiques, https://www.insee.fr/en/metadonnees/definition/c1361. [9]

Insee (2016), *Urban Area*, Institut national de la statistique et des études économiques, https://www.insee.fr/en/metadonnees/definition/c2070. [8]

Istat (2014), *Labour Market Areas 2014.* [10]

OECD (2018), *Survey OECD WPTI.* [2]

OECD (2002), *Redefining Territories: The Functional Regions*, OECD Publishing, Paris, https://dx.doi.org/10.1787/9789264196179-en. [1]

ONS (2019), *Boundaries of travel to work areas.* [7]

Silm, S. and R. Ahas (2010), "The seasonal variability of population in Estonian municipalities", *Environment and Planning*, Vol. A, pp. 2527-2546. [15]

Statistics Canada (2012), *Census Dictionary*, https://www12.statcan.gc.ca/census-recensement/2011/ref/dict/98-301-X2011001-eng.pdf. [4]

Tammaru, T., H. Kulu and I. Kask (2004), "Urbanization, suburbanization, and counterurbanization in Estonia", *Eurasian Geography and Economics*, Vol. 45/3, pp. 212-229. [16]

Chapter 4. Methodological guidelines to define functional areas

This chapter presents the methodology used to delineate functional areas in all types of territories based on multidirectional-flow data. It explains the underlying algorithms and discusses the importance of parameter selection for the results obtained by the method. The chapter provides a number of methodological guidelines that will help OECD countries to apply the concept of functional areas in their entire national territory.

The objective of this chapter is to outline one methodology to define functional areas that is replicable in different countries, based on functional criteria in terms of commuting flows and covers the entire national territory. The methodology follows the work of Coombes and Bond (2008[1]) using a multidirectional-flow-based approach. Functional areas cluster geographic units such that: i) the majority of people that work in the area also reside in the area; and ii) the majority of workers that live in the area also work in the area.

The first section of the chapter describes the methodology. The next sections provide guidelines to select the parameters and perform post-processing modifications. The final section describes two open-source software packages that are now available to national statistical offices (NSOs) and the research community for the delineation of functional areas in all territories. Thus, this chapter showcases how the delineation and mapping exercise can primarily use open-source computational packages and replicable methods already available in R[1] and Python,[2] in order to promote the modernisation of statistical systems.

A multidirectional-flow and bottom-up iterative process

The prevailing methodology to create self-contained functional areas is a bottom-up process that clusters geographic units iteratively on the basis of multidirectional mobility flows. In this context, bottom-up means that the process pairs a single geographic unit with another single geographic unit, forming a new cluster. The new cluster must satisfy criteria based on self-containment and possibly on size. Self-containment denotes the share of the labour force that lives and works in the area. Size refers to a minimum number of workers living in the area.

There are two measures of self-containment: supply-side self-containment (SSC) and demand-side self-containment (DSC). SSC is the number of people living and working in an area divided by the number of residents in the area. DSC is the number of people living and working in an area divided by the number of jobs in the area.

The methodology, described in Figure 4.1, pairs geographic units iteratively into clusters until all clusters satisfy the following criteria:

- The size of the cluster contains at least a minimum number of workers, W_{min}, that live in the cluster and the SSC and DSC are above a level self-containment, SC_{target}.

- If the size of the cluster exceeds a target number of workers, W_{target}, the rate of SSC and DSC must be above a level of self-containment, SC_{min}.

- If the number of employees in the cluster is between the minimum W_{min} and the target W_{target} amount of workers, the minimum level of self-containment SC_i should decrease from SC_{target} for smaller-size clusters to SC_{min} for bigger-sized clusters, see Figure 4.2.[3]

To start the process, the user decides on the parameters SC_{min}, SC_{target}, W_{min} and W_{target}. Using those parameters, the method first assigns a *distance from success* to each geographic unit through an algorithm explained in the annex. *Distance from success* is a quantitative measure of the distance to meeting the criteria specified above. Next, the algorithm selects the geographic unit with the farthest *distance from success*. Then, the algorithm pairs the unit selected with another geographic unit or cluster. A pairing algorithm (see annex) measures the strength of the relationship between two geographic units and accounts for the relative importance of commuting flows and employment between the units. Following this step, the algorithm returns a new cluster, consisting of geographic units with the strongest relationship.

In the third and final step, the method tests if the new cluster satisfies the requirements of size and self-containment. This process iterates until the clusters meet the conditions to be categorised as a functional area or the maximum number of iterations is reached.

Figure 4.1. Steps to create functional areas

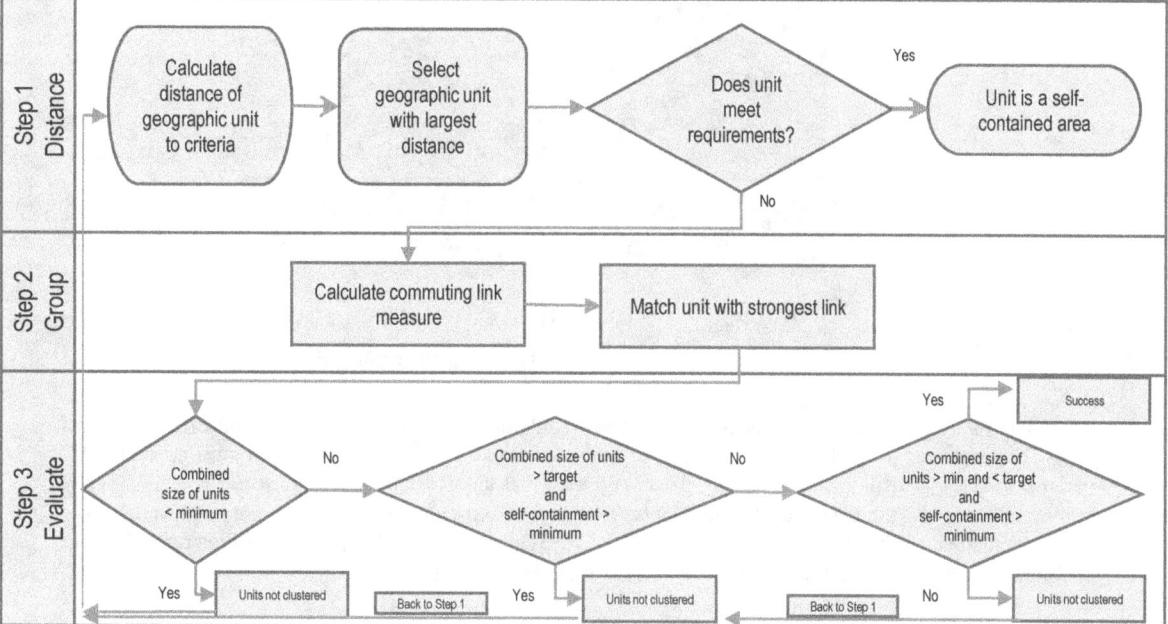

Source: Fadic, M., L. Kleine-Rueschkamp and P. Veneri (2019[2]), "Functional areas for all territories".

The importance of parameter selection

The boundaries of functional areas depend on the selection and calibration of the four parameters relating to size and self-containment. These parameters allow users to adapt the methodology to different commuting patterns, units of measurements and size of municipalities.

The minimum and target number of employees in the area, W_{min} and W_{target}, can be used to ensure that the size of functional areas is useful for statistical purposes and captures integrated areas. The minimum SC_{min} and target SC_{target} levels of self-containment determine the total number of functional areas. A higher SC_{min} will lower the number of functional areas whereas a lower threshold will tend to increase the number of functional areas.

Figure 4.2. Self-containment requirements for functional areas

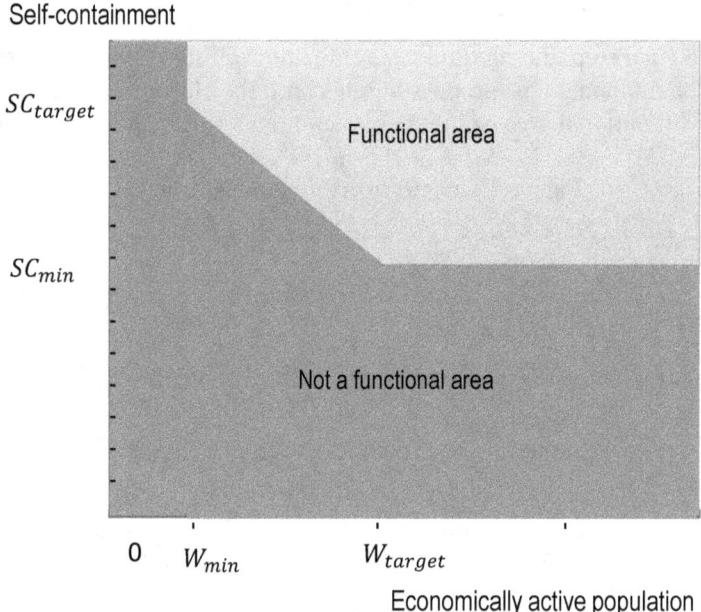

Note: The figure above shows the requirements of self-containment and size for the creation of a functional area. The parameter W_{min} denotes the minimum number of workers that a functional area must contain. The parameter SC_{target} denotes the level of self-containment that an area with W_{min} must meet to satisfy the criteria. Conversely, the parameter SC_{min} denotes the level of self-containment that an area with more than W_{target} must have. The slope between the points (W_{min}, SC_{target}) and (W_{target}, SC_{min}) illustrates that the self-containment requirement decreases as the size of the area increases.

Functional areas should identify clusters of geographic units that are integrated socially and economically. As such, the choice of parameter-values depends on country-specific characteristics. Nonetheless, the following principles serve as general guidelines to create comparable cross-country functional areas:[4]

1. **Whereas the parameters SC_{min} and SC_{target} should be comparable across countries; the parameters W_{min} and W_{target} should be used to capture country-specific characteristics.**

   The choice of parameters depends on country-specific requirements. In the application exercises, the chosen values for the parameters SC_{min} and SC_{target} ranged from 0.7 to 0.75 and 0.9 to 0.95 respectively. Such high values for SC_{target} are needed in countries where large areas show low population density (such as Canada and some parts of the United States). However, lower values are sufficient when this situation is not common (this is the case for Italy and the United Kingdom). Moreover, to avoid the spreading of densely populated municipalities into lower density surrounding areas, lower values of the parameter SC_{min} can be used (see Italy and the UK). To ensure that identified functional areas truly capture labour market links, the self-containment parameter should be no less than 0.5. In any case, the chosen levels of the self-containment parameter are the minimum thresholds for the algorithm. Only a very small proportion of the functional areas (FAs) should have values as low as these minimum values. The large majority of FAs at the end of the delineation process will present higher values of self-containment with respect to the initial choice. To ensure international comparability, it might be recommendable to ensure that the vast majority of FAs show values of self-containment higher than 0.7.

2. **The maximum population of a functional area should normally not be larger than the corresponding population of the territorial level 3 unit (TL3 regions).**

    Functional areas capture integrated areas and should not exceed corresponding TL3 regions in size, as these are generally a country's second-tier administrative division. Functional areas bigger than TL3 regions may be too large to capture important economic and labour market linkages. However, in some cases having labour market areas comparable in size to TL3 regions can help collect solid territorial statistics as for instance in the European Union (EU) regarding data from social surveys.

The countries of Canada and Mexico serve as appropriate examples to illustrate the importance of parameter selection and calibration. Suppose a researcher wants to use the methodology to create functional areas in both countries using the census subdivisions (CSDs) for Canada and municipalities for Mexico. Canada is divided into 5 163 CSDs (2016 Census of Population of Canada) with an average of around 3 000 employees. Mexico has 2 446 municipalities (2015) with an average of 18 000 employees. The country-specific differences imply that using the same parameters for both countries might not yield comparable results. In one country, the functional areas may provide no meaningful agglomerations whereas, in the other, the functional areas may be too big for statistical purposes.

Coherence with other existing statistical areas

Functional areas can complement existing administrative and statistical areas. In cases where the country has an existing national core-based definition of functional areas (i.e. functional urban areas, metropolitan statistical areas, census metropolitan areas, etc.), it is recommendable to make multidirectional functional area clusters coherent with those existing functional boundaries. This implies that the delineation algorithms should retain the shape and integrity of existing statistical areas. To exclude existing statistical areas, the commuting flows (inflow and outflow) of the geographic units belonging to these areas should be set to zero.

Post-processing

Following the creation of functional areas, the next step is the post-processing of the results. Post-processing identifies strong deviations from regular patterns such as isolation and non-contiguity issues that may occur due to commuting flow data issues or geographic isolation of units.

Post-processing resolves each anomaly by using country-specific knowledge such as statistical hierarchies and past commuting data to ensure that functional areas are relevant and cover the entire territory. The main corrections in the post-processing stage are:

1. **Merging of functional areas**

    The merging of functional areas may be required in cases where the functional area is composed of a few geographic units. This may occur if, for instance, a municipality has no commuting flows and therefore all workers live in the same place they work. At the same time, it is possible to have geographic units that consist of few municipalities but represent an area of interest. For this reason, the following aspects should be considered when deciding whether to merge functional areas:

- Setting threshold values on the size of a functional area to determine whether it should be merged is highly context-specific. In different countries, different thresholds might be applied. Furthermore, the choice of the size threshold will depend on whether functional urban areas (FUAs) are included in the delineation or not. For example, if a functional area consists of a small number of geographic units and their total population is larger than or comparable to the average population of all functional areas in the country, then it might be best not to merge the functional area.

- In all other cases, the functional area should be merged with the closest functional area. To this purpose, distance or commuting flows may be used to measure closeness.

2. Treating isolated and unassigned functional areas

Unassigned functional areas are functional areas that contain only one geographic unit (building block). Isolated functional areas do not share a border with other functional areas. Both anomalies may occur due to a lack of commuting towards other units (such as islands or overseas territories) or data availability issues.

In both cases, the user must determine if the functional area should be integrated into the closest functional area. To this purpose, the user can rely on commuting flows to the functional areas or administrative divisions if such commuting flows to other areas exist.

3. Disjoint functional areas

In certain cases, the commuting flows will join geographic units that are non-contiguous. In this case, the functional area will be disjoint and might cross administrative subdivisions. This may occur in instances where non-traditional commuting flow sources are used, such as mobile network data. In these cases, a custom solution must be devised.

Transparency through open source

The use of open-source software allows interested parties to reproduce, validate and evaluate the methodology discussed in this chapter. There are two main open-source repositories currently available to create functional areas using commuting data. The open-source algorithms follow Coombes and Bond (2008[1]) and are available in the open-source programming languages R and Python. For R, the Italian National Institute of Statistics (Istat) developed the library LabourMarketAreas (Franconi et al., 2017[3]).[5] For Python, Statistics Canada is currently developing the *self-contained labour areas* (SLAs) library[6] (Alasia, 2016[4]). The two packages are very similar in nature and based on the same algorithm; nevertheless, they present minor differences in the clustering process, as well as differences in the way they could be adapted to specific data configurations.

Consultation or user feedback

Consultation and feedback from potential users of functional areas, i.e. policymakers and statistical offices, are highly important. They raise awareness on the issue of territorial linkages and can also contribute to wider public acceptance of delineated functional areas. A key challenge consists of highlighting the positive value added of functional areas for identifying territorial linkages and possible policy challenges while acknowledging pre-established administrative units that serve in most countries as the main areas for policymaking.

Notes

[1] The R library LabourMarketAreas contains the relevant code and was made available by Istat in 2018.

[2] Statistics Canada developed a Python code, released in PyPI, the Python Package Index, that complements the R programme for delineating functional areas. This code is available at https://pypi.org/project/SLA-ZTA/. As discussed in more detail in the technical appendix, they are conceptually similar but present some differences in the way the clustering process is implemented.

[3] The parameters SC_{min}, SC_{target}, W_{min} and W_{target} can be calibrated to adapt to country-specific contexts. In the application of this methodology for the United Kingdom, Coombes and Bond (2008[1]) select 3 500 for W_{min}, 25 000 for W_{target}, 75% and 66.6% for SC_{target} and SC_{min} respectively.

[4] The principles are derived from the authors' analysis and follow consultations with the project's scientific committee.

[5] https://CRAN.R-project.org/package=LabourMarketAreas; the description of the package is available at https://cran.r-project.org/web/packages/LabourMarketAreas/LabourMarketAreas.pdf. The technical paper is presented in Franconi et al. (2018[5]).

[6] See https://pypi.org/project/SLA-ZTA/.

References

Alasia, A. (2016), "Operationalizing 'Self-contained Labour Areas' as a potential standard geography for disseminating Statistics Canada data", Presentation. [4]

Coombes, M. and S. Bond (2008), *Travel-to-work Areas: The 2007 Review*, Office for National Statistics, London. [1]

Fadic, M., L. Kleine-Rueschkamp and P. Veneri (2019), "Functional areas for all territories". [2]

Franconi, D. et al. (2018), *Istat Implementation of the Algorithm to Develop Labour Market Areas*, 3.2.2, https://cran.r-project.org/web/packages/LabourMarketAreas/. [5]

Franconi, L. et al. (2017), "Guidelines for Labour Market Area delineation process: From definition to dissemination", Istat. [3]

Chapter 5. Applying existing methods to countries without established functional areas

This chapter uses the method for delineating functional areas explained and discussed in Chapter 4. It applies the method in five OECD countries that so far have no fully established functional area geography for their entire national territory. The chapter presents the application results for each country. Additionally, the chapter illustrates how non-traditional data sources such as mobile phone data can help identify functional linkages between different areas.

Several OECD countries have not yet developed a comprehensive definition of functional areas for their entire territory. This chapter applies existing methods for delineating functional areas, presented in Chapter 4, to the following five OECD member countries for illustrative and research purposes: Canada, Estonia, Korea, Mexico and the United States. In pursuing this exercise, the report does not aim to create or impose new statistical conventions but rather tries to illustrate the methodology application. Canada was chosen due to Statistics Canada's ongoing work to define functional areas. The United States was picked for comparative reasons (similar geography and geographic challenges to Canada) and research purposes. The analysis includes Korea and Mexico, as both are populous OECD countries that so far have not established functional area geographies for their entire national territories. Estonia is part of the application exercise to demonstrate how unconventional data sources, in this case, mobile phone data, can provide the necessary information to delineate functional areas.

There are two maps available for each country. The first map presents the results of the exercise taking into account all geographic units in the country. The second map excludes the geographic units that also form part of a functional urban area (FUA). The libraries used to create the functional areas are Python's self-contained labour areas (SLAs) for Canada and the United States and R's LabourMarketAreas for all other countries.

Table 5.1 provides an overview of the application results in the five countries considered. It reports the number of identified functional areas, their average size in terms of incorporated administrative units and their average population size. Additionally, it specifies the parameter values in terms of population size and self-containment that yielded the estimation results. Furthermore, the table shows how those summary statistics change if FUAs are excluded and the delineation of functional areas thus only covers the remaining territory.

Table 5.1. Summary of results

Scenario	W_{min} (000s)	W_{target} (000s)	SC_{min} (%)	SC_{target} (%)	Number of areas	Avg. units per cluster	Avg. population	FUA included
Estonia	10	20	70	95	17	50	82 214	No
Estonia	10	20	70	95	16	53	87 353	Yes
Korea	100	300	70	95	48	5	897 811	No
Korea	100	300	75	90	36	6	1 197 083	Yes
Mexico	50	100	75	90	228	11	555 635	No
Mexico	50	100	75	90	186	13	681 102	Yes
United States	0	25	70	95	882	4	370 000	No
United States	0	25	70	95	762	4	426 900	Yes
Canada	0	15	75	90	440	8	12 300	No
Canada	0	15	75	90	337	10	103 800	Yes

Note: The table above provides summary statistics of the delineation of functional areas for selected OECD member and OECD accession countries. W_{min} and W_{target} denote the minimum and target number of employees in the area respectively. SC_{min} and SC_{target} denote the minimum and target levels of self-containment respectively. The column FUA indicates if statistical areas were included in the exercise. Size refers to population size of the functional areas.

Canada

Statistics Canada developed the geography of SLAs that covers all Canadian municipalities using commuting data. Each SLA consists of a self-contained grouping of areas where the majority of residents both work and live.

The SLAs use census subdivision (CSD) data from the 2006 Census of Population and the 2011 National Household Survey as building blocks. Currently, Statistics Canada is updating the SLA geography based on the 2016 Census of Population data. CSDs in Canada are heterogeneous in size and population.

A key question in the process to create SLAs is the integration of the functional area methods with the existing Census Metropolitan Area/Census Agglomeration (CMA/CA) geography. Consequently, three main options were explored to delineate functional areas for the entire territory. The first maintains the parameters for the SLA geography without consideration of the CMA/CA areas. The second examines potential adjustments to the choice of the parameters in the SLA method to achieve better alignment with CMAs/CAs. The final option delineating SLAs while only using commuting flows between non-CMA/CA areas.

Statistics Canada determined that the best option appeared to be redoing the SLA geography while only including commuting flows among non-CMA/CA areas. This option has two major advantages: it offers an alignment between SLAs and CMAs/CAs and it nonetheless provides useful information on areas outside CMAs/CAs that constitute meaningful non-urban or rural labour markets. However, the option of starting with the "fixed" FUAs (CMAs/CAs) and then only running a multi-directional analysis on the remaining areas might also create some problems. For example, Figure 5.2 shows some isolated small areas outside the FUAs in southern Ontario.

Figure 5.1 presents the territory containing CMAs/CAs before delineating SLAs for Eastern Canada. Figure 5.2 presents the SLAs developed using the methodology. The figures provide insights into how SLAs outside CMAs/CAs form and which census subdivisions make up the respective cluster.

Figure 5.1. 2016 Census metropolitan areas (CMAs), 2016 census agglomerations (CAs) and 2016 census subdivisions (CSDs), Eastern Canada

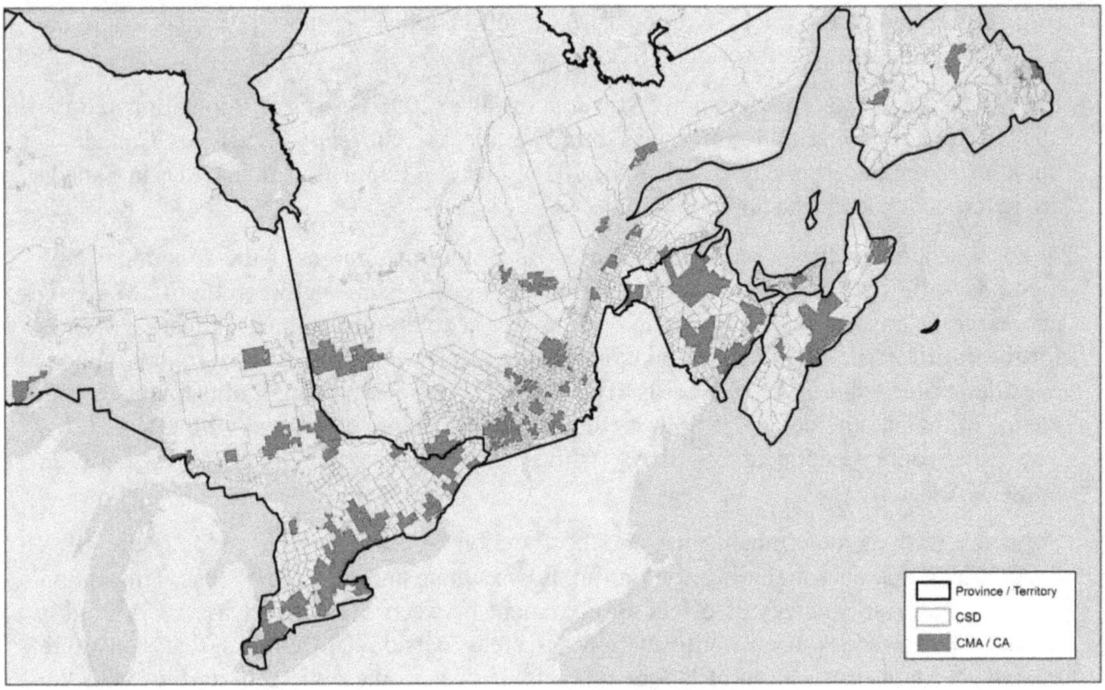

Source: Statistics Canada, 2019.

Figure 5.2. 2016 Census metropolitan areas (CMAs), 2016 census agglomerations (CAs) and self-contained labour areas (SLAs), Eastern Canada

Source: Statistics Canada, 2019.

United States

For the purposes of research and comparison to Canadian areas, the methodology was applied to the United States. The building blocks to create functional areas (FAs) in the United States are the counties. The United States has 3 220 counties with an average number of employees of 45 000. The data for the United States come from the five-year (2011-15) American Community Survey Commuting Flows.

Counties in the United States are heterogeneous in size and population. The population in counties range from a few thousand up to around 10 million people and are not equally distributed.[1]

Figure 5.3 presents the estimated functional areas for all counties in the United States using the following parameters: SC_{min} 70%, SC_{target} 95%, W_{min} 0, W_{target} 25 000. Figure 5.4 shows the estimated functional areas excluding the counties that belong to a functional urban area.

Figure 5.3. Functional areas (FAs) in the United States

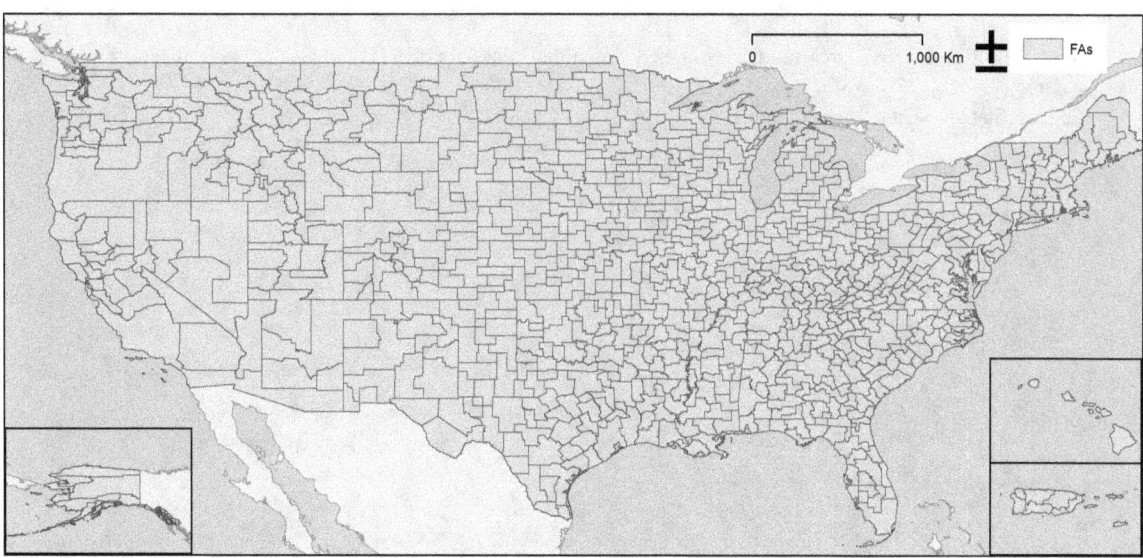

Note: The figure above presents the estimated functional areas for the United States using the following parameters: SC_{min} 70%, SC_{target} 95%, W_{min} 0, W_{target} 25 000.
Source: Statistics Canada calculations.

Figure 5.4. Functional areas (FAs) and functional urban areas (FUAs) in the United States

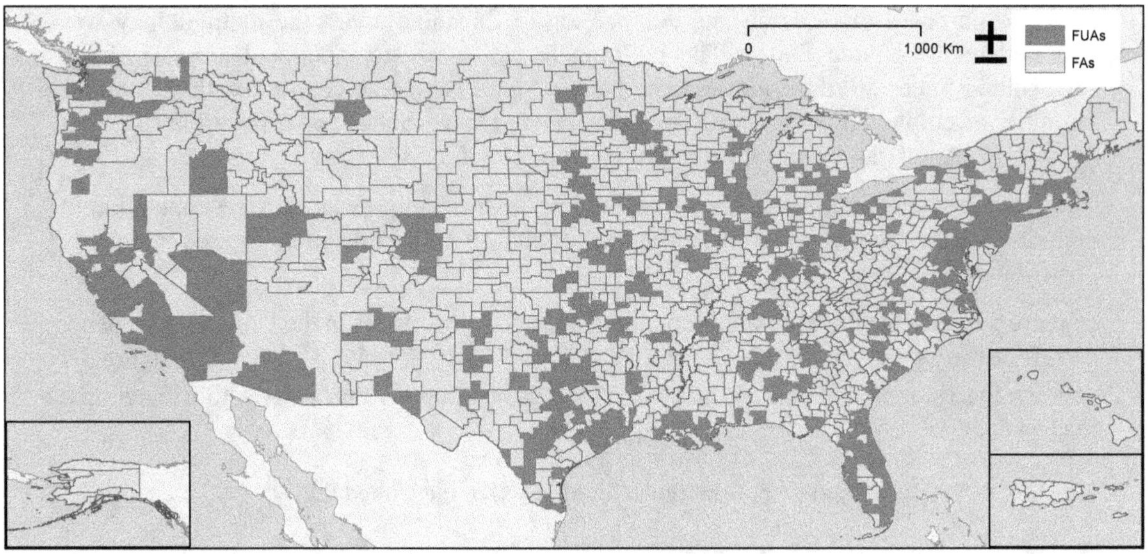

Note: The figure above presents the estimated functional areas for the United States using the following parameters: SC_{min} 70%, SC_{target} 95%, W_{min} 0, W_{target} 25 000.
Source: Statistics Canada calculations.

Mexico

The building blocks to create functional areas (FAs) in Mexico are the municipalities. Mexico has 2 446 municipalities (2015) with an average number of employees of approximately 18 000. The commuting flow data come from the 2015 census.

Municipalities in Mexico are heterogeneous in size and population. Municipalities in the northern part of the country tend to be bigger in size than municipalities in the middle of the country. Furthermore, some municipalities such as Ensenada encompass an entire TL3 region, the second-largest administrative division of the country.

Figure 5.5 presents the estimated functional areas for all municipalities in Mexico using the following parameters: SC_{min} 75%, SC_{target} 90%, W_{min} 50 000, W_{target} 100 000. Figure 5.6 shows the estimated functional areas excluding the municipalities that belong to a functional urban area.

Figure 5.5. Functional areas (FAs) in Mexico

Note: The figure above presents the estimated functional areas for Mexico using the following parameters: SC_{min} 75%, SC_{target} 90%, W_{min} 50 000, W_{target} 100 000. Results shown are post-processing.
Source: OECD calculations.

Figure 5.6. Functional areas (FAs) and functional urban areas (FUAs) in Mexico

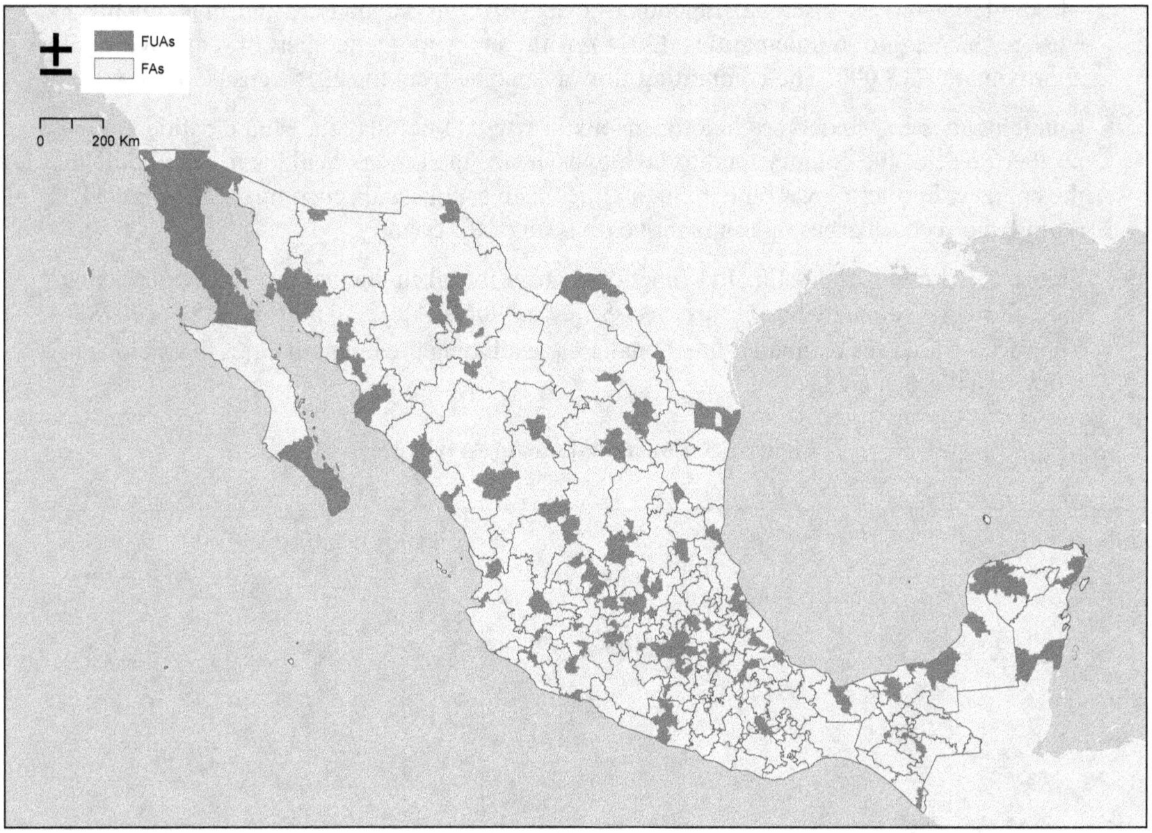

Note: The figure above presents the estimated functional areas for Mexico using the following parameters: SC_{min} 75%, SC_{target} 90%, W_{min} 50 000, W_{target} 100 000. Results shown are post-processing.
Source: OECD calculations.

Korea

The building block to create functional areas (FAs) in Korea are the municipalities. There are a total of 227 municipalities (2015) with an average of approximately 130 000 employees. The commuting flow data come from the population census and was provided by Statistics Korea.

Municipalities in Korea are larger in population and density than the geographic units for other countries examined in this report. To account for these differences, the parameters W_{min} and W_{target} have a higher threshold.

Figure 5.7 presents the estimated functional areas for all municipalities in Korea using the following parameters: SC_{min} 75%, SC_{target} 90%, W_{min} 100 000, W_{target} 300 000. Figure 5.8 presents the estimated functional areas excluding the municipalities that belong to a functional urban area. Similar to the case of Canada, excluding FUAs from the delineation of functional areas might yield some problems. For instance, in Korea, that second approach shows a "donut" functional area defined around Chuncheon (Figure 5.8).

Figure 5.7. Functional areas (FAs) in Korea

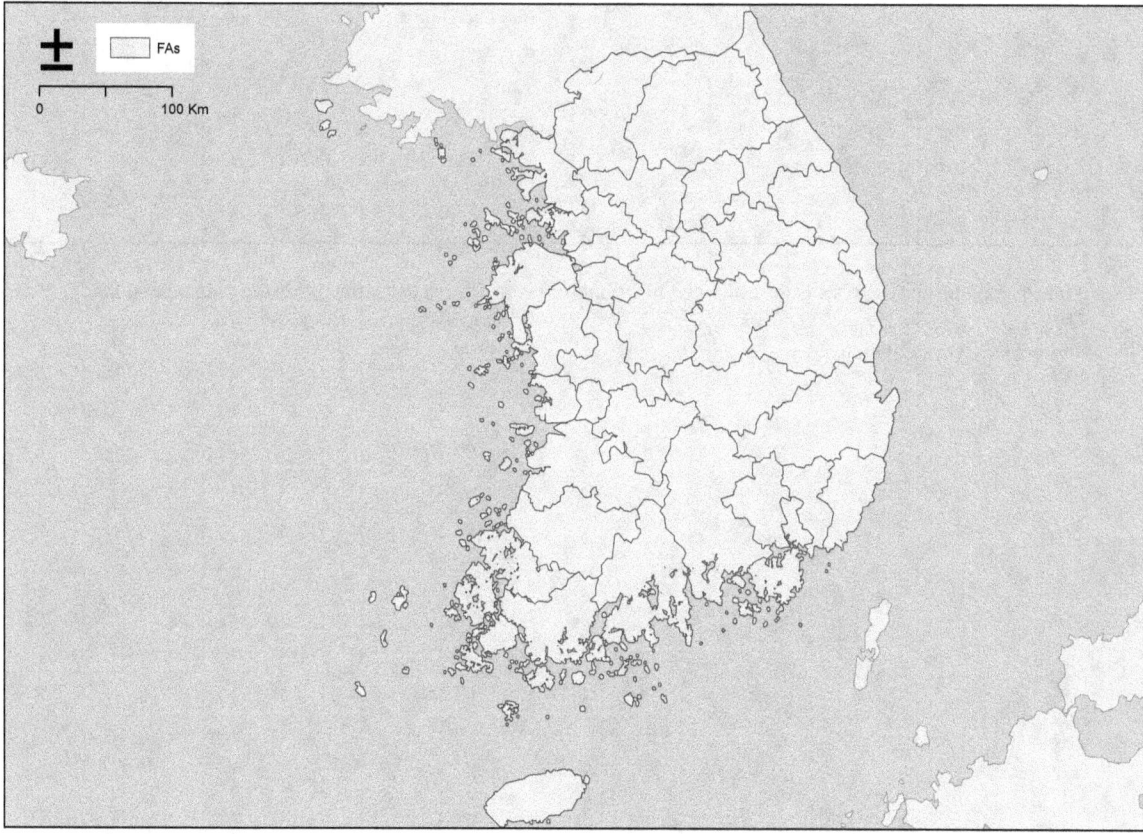

Note: The figure above presents the estimated functional areas for Korea using the following parameters: SC_{min} 75%, SC_{target} 90%, W_{min} 100 000, W_{target} 300 000. Results shown are post-processing.
Source: OECD calculations.

Figure 5.8. Functional areas (FAs) and functional urban areas (FUAs) in Korea

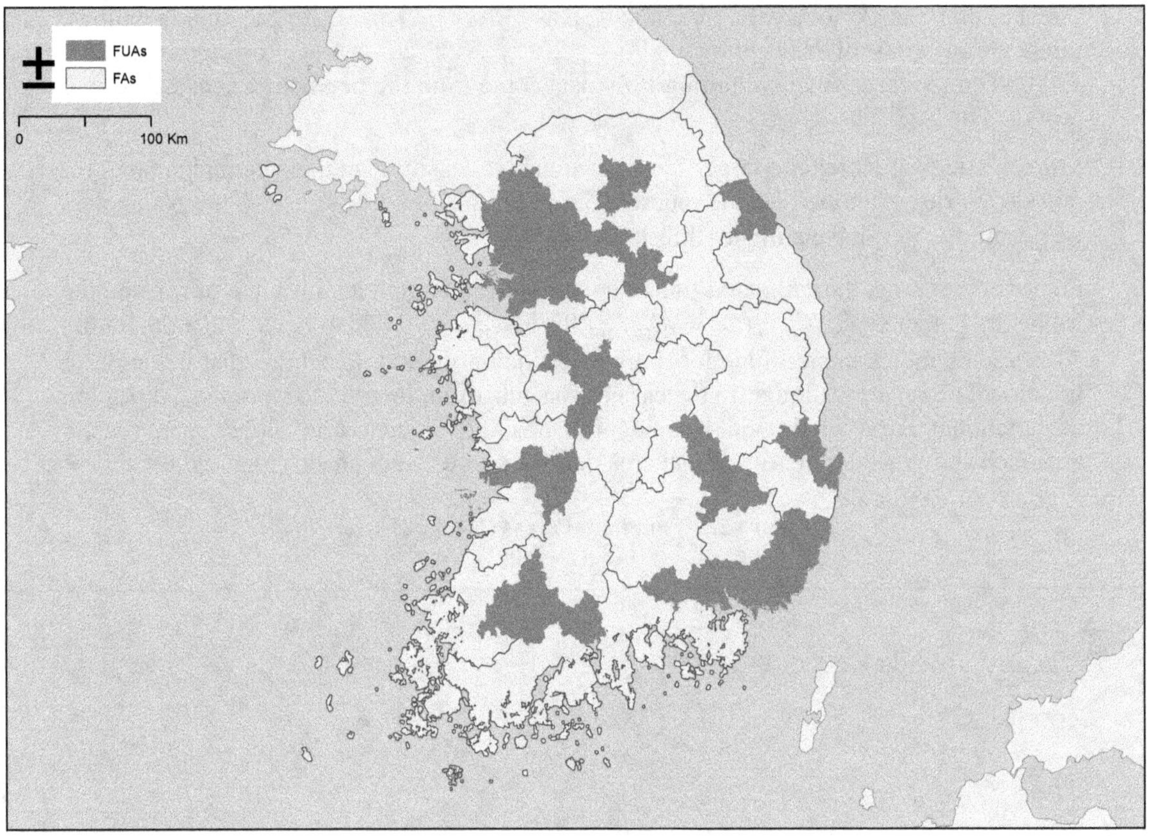

Note: The figure above presents the estimated functional areas for Korea using the following parameters: SC_{min} 75%, SC_{target} 90%, W_{min} 100 000, W_{target} 300 000. Results shown are post-processing.
Source: OECD calculations.

Estonia

The building blocks to create functional areas (FAs) in Estonia are the territorial communities. There are a total of 847 territorial communities across the country with an average population of approximately 1 650 inhabitants.

The commuting flow data are derived from mobile positioning data, provided by Aasa (2019[1]). In contrast to other data sources examined, the data for Estonia provide estimates of commuting flows for the entire population (not only employees) at a highly disaggregated level.

The pre-processed results in Estonia contained several non-contiguous and disjoint functional areas. This may be due to the low population of some geographic units, the interconnectivity of geographic areas and the small size of the country. The post-processing algorithms re-assigned isolated and disjoint functional areas following the methodological guidelines discussed in Chapter 5.

Figure 5.9 presents the estimated functional areas for all territorial communities in Estonia using the following parameters: SC_{min} 70%, SC_{target} 95%, W_{min} 10 000, W_{target} 20 000. Figure 5.10 presents the estimated functional areas excluding the territorial communities that belong to a functional urban area.

Figure 5.9. Functional areas (FA) in Estonia

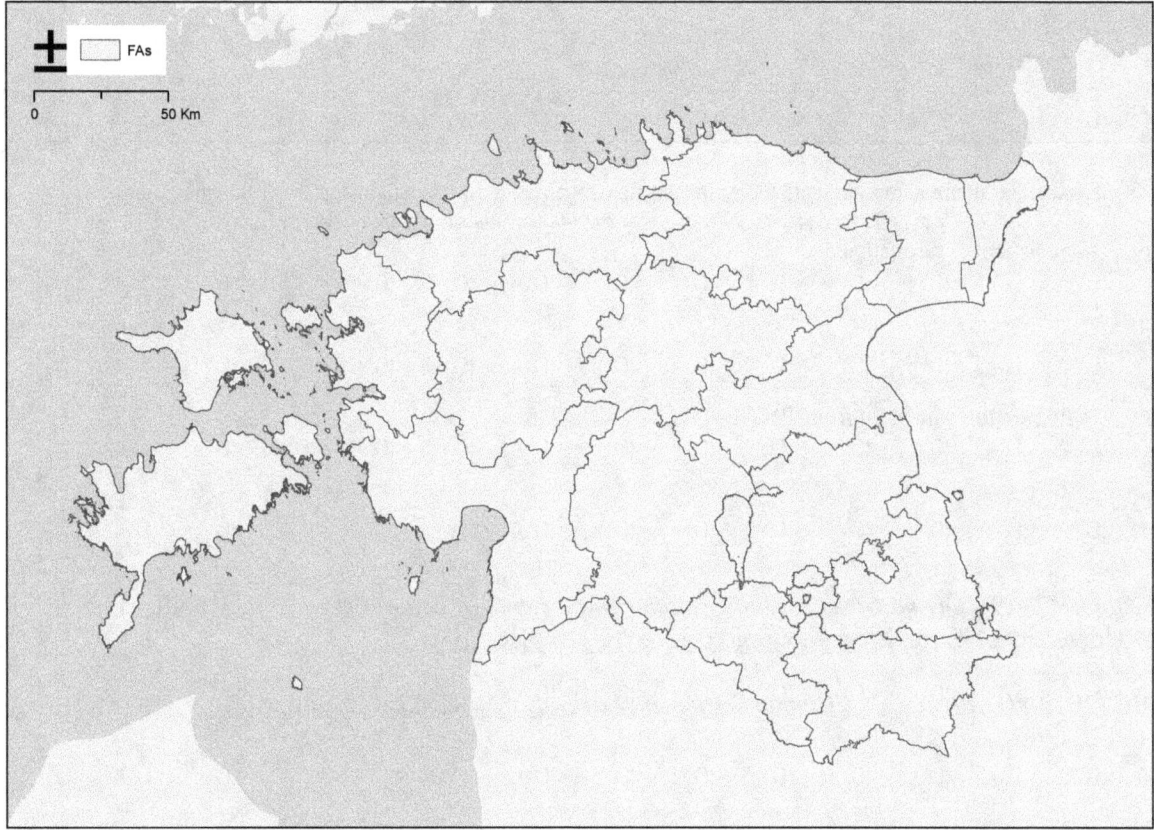

Note: The figure above presents the estimated functional areas for Estonia using the following parameters: SC_{min} 70%, SC_{target} 95%, W_{min} 10 000, W_{target} 20 000. Results shown are post-processing.
Source: OECD calculations.

Figure 5.10. Functional areas (FA) and functional urban areas (FUAs) in Estonia

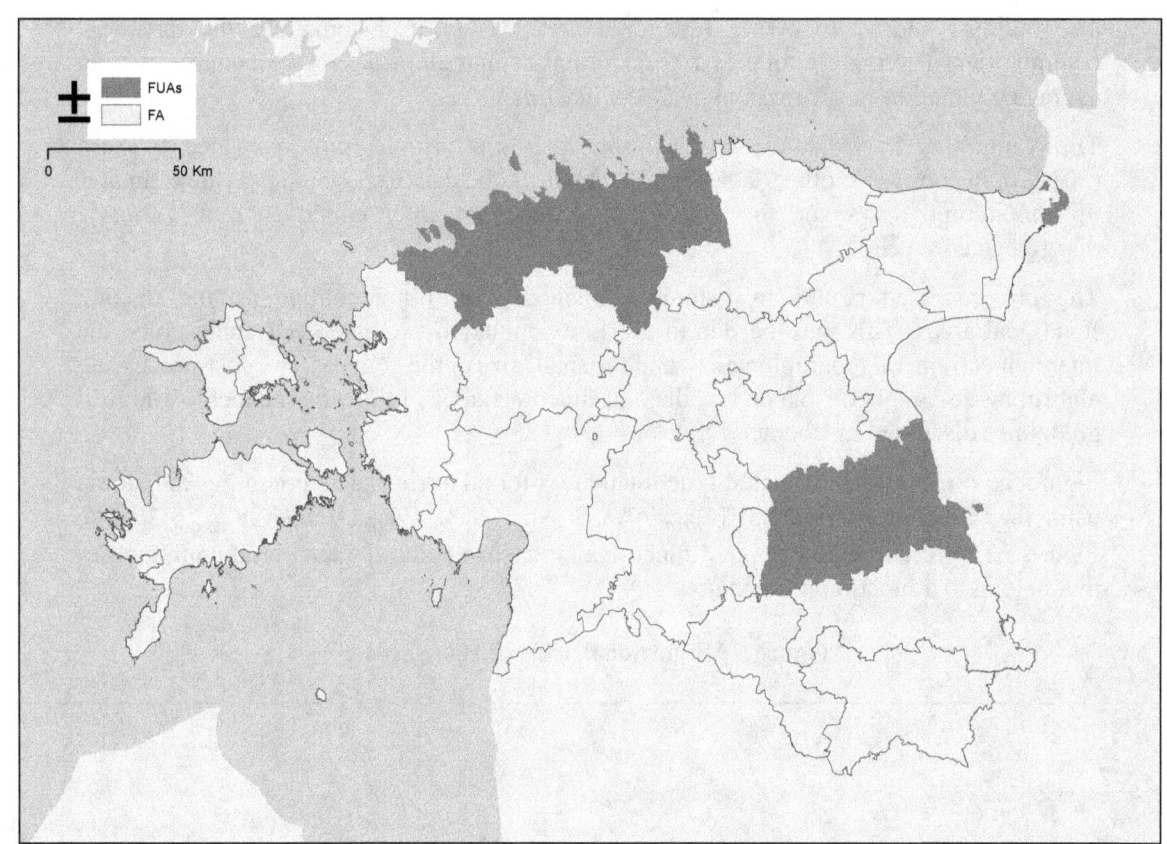

Note: The figure above presents the estimated functional areas for Estonia using the following parameters: SC_{min} 70%, SC_{target} 95%, W_{min} 10 000, W_{target} 20 000. Results shown are post-processing.
Source: OECD calculations.

Note

[1] Population data stem from JRC (2019[2]).

References

Aasa, A. (2019), *OD-matrices of Daily Regular Movements in Estonia (Dataset)*, Mobility Lab, University of Tartu, https://doi.org/10.23659/UTMOBLAB-1. [1]

JRC (2019), *GHSL - Global Human Settlement Layer*, https://ghsl.jrc.ec.europa.eu/. [2]

Conclusion

Economic, territorial linkages are an important factor in both statisticians' and regional development policy makers' work and decisions. In considering the connection between different areas and their economic and social interdependence, policy makers can target policies at the right geographic scale that takes into account such interconnectedness. The concept of functional areas, or local labour market areas, offers exactly this consideration of territorial linkages by identifying close labour market links, through commuting flows, between different geographic units and different types of settlements.

Due to the advantage of taking into account geographies that reflect the territorial linkages created by the daily movement of people, various OECD countries have identified and established functional areas for statistical and policy-making purposes. However, these functional geographies are often limited to cities and their area of economic influence (e.g. commuting zone) even though functional areas exist in all types of territories, rural and urban alike. Therefore, this report offers a fresh examination of existing practices, reviews the policy relevance of functional areas and provides methodological guidelines as well as an experimental mapping exercise that illustrate how functional areas can be delineated in all types of territories.

While functional areas might not be suitable for all statistical purposes, they can complement territorial statistics on administrative units. No specific geographic unit, including functional areas and administrative areas, is ideal for all types of spatial analyses. Instead, the most appropriate geography depends on the purpose of each specific analysis. Consequently, functional areas can enrich both policy design and territorial statistics, especially in terms of assessing and designing policies for labour market areas that do not correspond to traditional geographies. Even though the method applied in this report builds on commuting-to-work flows, which primarily provide a key measure of the extent of local labour markets, it can also delineate a reference geography for improving the efficiency and organisation of service provision in different types of areas.

In reviewing and applying methods to delineate functional areas, this report also makes a twofold contribution to the modernisation of statistical systems. First, it demonstrates how functional geographies can be identified or extended to a country's entire national territory with open-source software, building on transparent and replicable methods. Second, the report illustrates how novel, unconventional data sources present promising opportunities to enrich traditional statistics and can inform both the creation of territorial indicators and the delineation of functional geographies.

Annex A. Country examples: EU country delineations of functional areas

This section visually presents the set of delineated labour market areas in four European Union countries that participated in the grant exercise on labour market areas issued by Eurostat. The chosen experimental approach identified 83 functional areas in Hungary (Figure A A.1), 311 functional areas in Finland (Figure A A.2), 103 in Bulgaria (Figure A A.3), and 25 in Portugal (Figure A A.4).

Figure A A.1. Labour market areas in Hungary

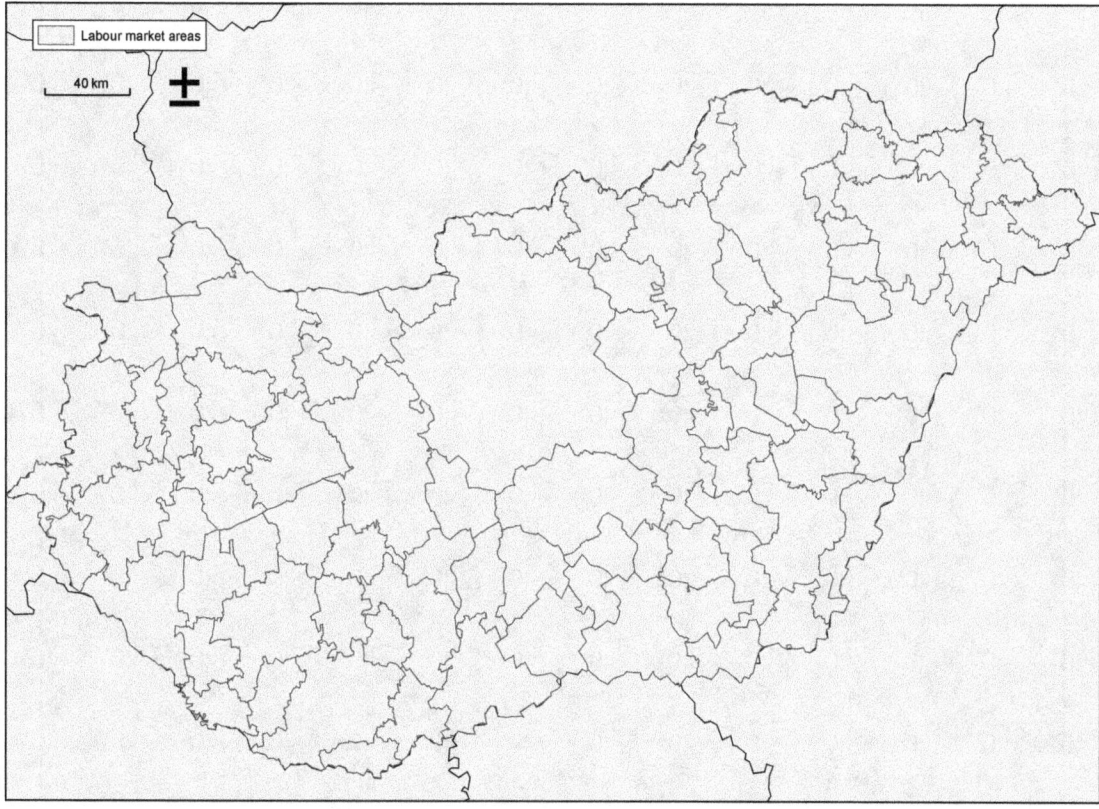

Note: The labour market areas for Hungary are based on 2011 commuting data.
Source: Eurostat (2015), *Harmonised Labour Market Areas*.

Figure A A.2. Experimental labour market areas in Finland

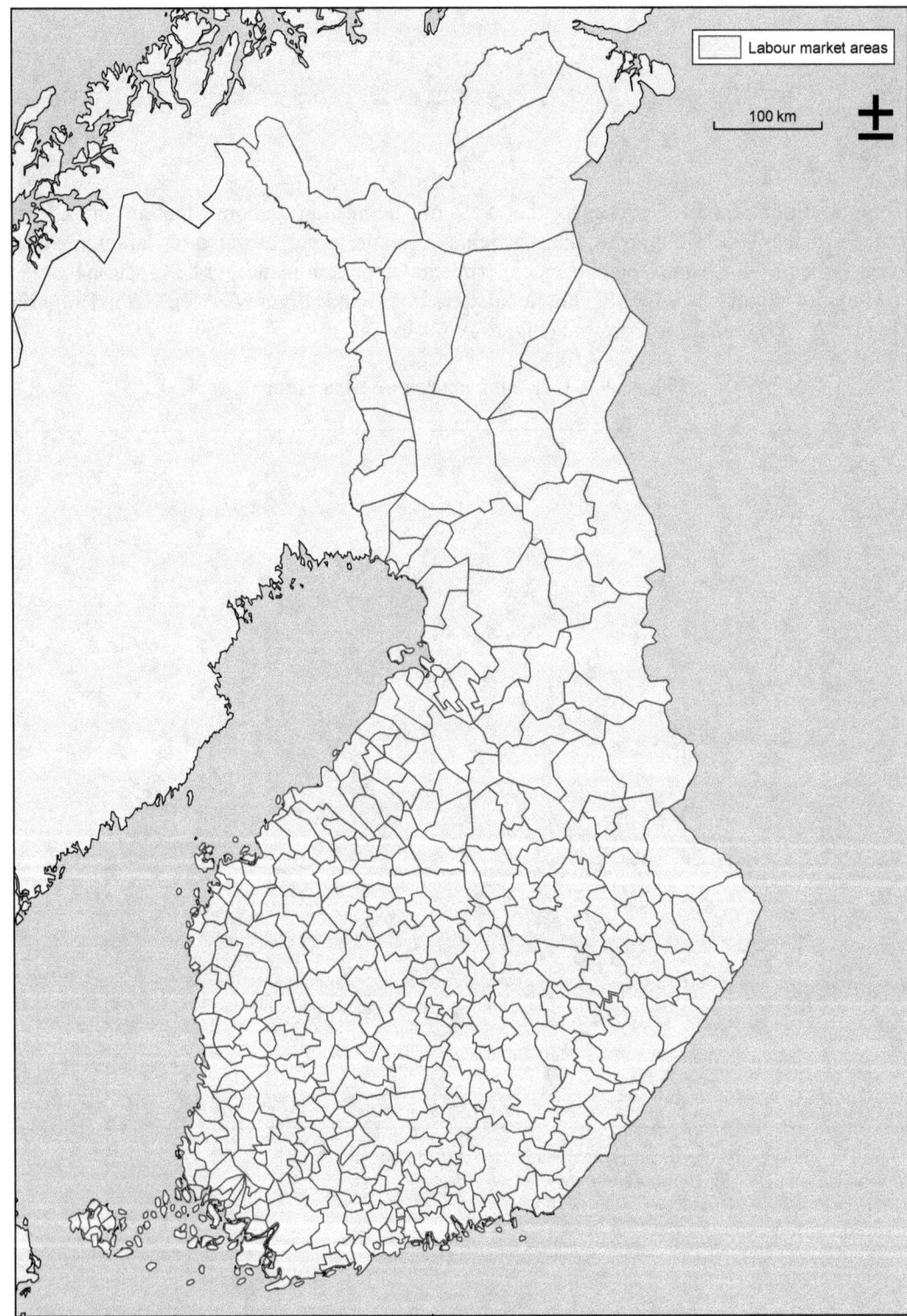

Note: The figure provides the 2018 experimental labour market areas for Finland using two types of building blocks – municipalities and postal areas. The parameters used are: SC_{min} 66%, SC_{target} 90%, W_{min} 3 000, W_{target} 40 000.
Source: Eurostat (2015), *Harmonised Labour Market Areas*.

Figure A A.3. Labour market areas in Bulgaria

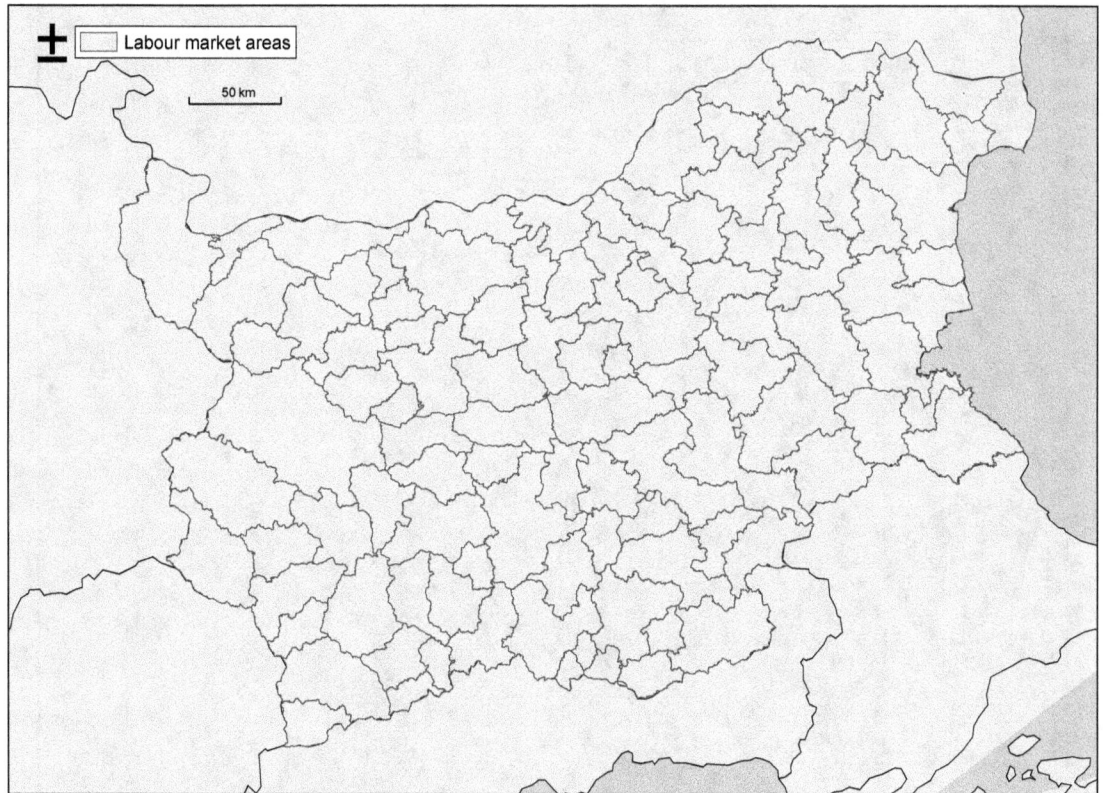

Note: The labour market areas for Bulgaria are based on 2011 commuting data.
Source: Eurostat (2015), *Harmonised Labour Market Areas*.

Figure A A.4. Labour market areas in Portugal

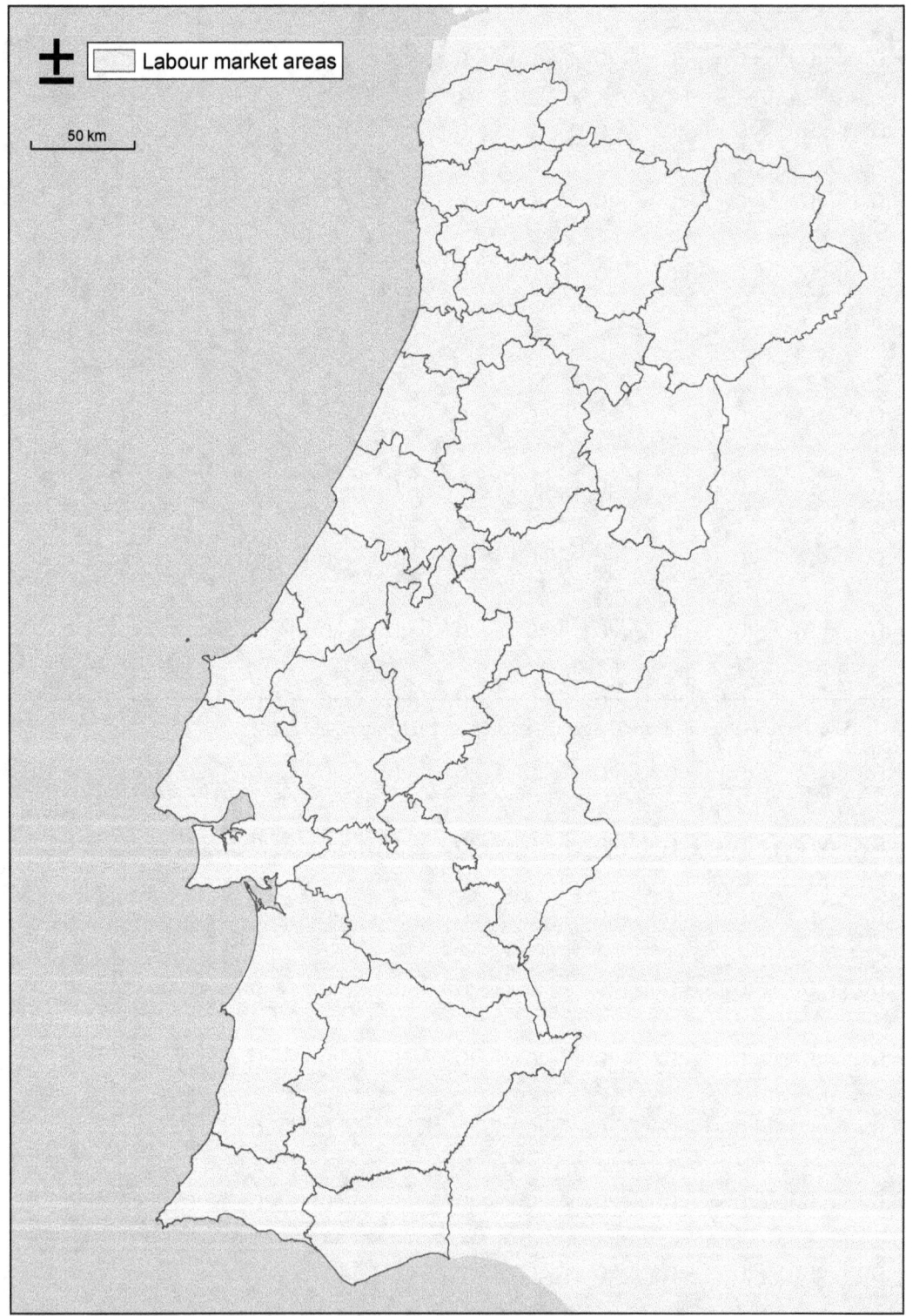

Note: The labour market areas for Portugal are based on 2011 commuting data.
Source: Eurostat (2015), *Harmonised Labour Market Areas*.

Annex B. Methodological algorithms

The following section describes the distance from success and search strength algorithm discussed in Chapter 5.

Distances from success

To calculate the quantitative distance between a cluster or geographic unit from the measurement criteria, the following formula is used:

- If the Resident Employed Labour Force is lower than the minimum population, then the distance is defined as:

$$Distance = \sqrt{(HS - RELF)^2 + (LP - RELF)^2} + \sqrt{(HS - WELF)^2 + (LP - WELF)^2}$$

- If the Resident Employed Labour Force is higher than the target population, then the distance is defined as:

$$Distance = \min\left\{\left(MS - \frac{RW}{REFL}\right), 0\right\} + \min\left\{\left(MS - \frac{RW}{WELF}\right), 0\right\}$$

In the R package, the distance from success is called validity and the following formula is used:

$$V(SC, W) = \left[1 - \left(1 - \frac{SC_{min}}{SC_{target}}\right) \cdot \max\left(\frac{W_{target} - W}{W_{target} - W_{min}}, 0\right)\right] \cdot \left[\frac{\min(SC, SC_{target})}{SC_{target}}\right]$$

$$V(SC, W) \geq \frac{SC_{min}}{SC_{target}}$$

Where W is the number of workers that live in the cluster and SC is the minimum self-containment (between SSC and DSC) of the cluster.

Search strength

The search strengths between two geographic units, A and B is calculated based on the commuting flows between A to B $F_{\{a,b\}}$ and from B to A $F_{\{b,a\}}$ the number of workers that live in area A $R_{\{a\}}$ and B $W_{\{b\}}$, and the number of workers that are resident in area A $W_{\{A\}}$ and B $R_{\{B\}}$.

$$Strength = \frac{F_{\{a,b\}}}{R_{\{a\}}} * \frac{F_{\{a,b\}}}{W_{\{b\}}} + \frac{F_{\{b,a\}}}{R_{\{b\}}} * \frac{F_{\{b,a\}}}{W_{\{a\}}}$$

Annex C. LabourMarketAreas – R package

The R package LabourMarketAreas implements the whole labour market area (LMA) delineation process and has a modular structure. It consists of a series of functions; each function addresses a specific stage of the LMA delineation process. In the subsequent section, a basic example of a typical delineation process is summarised. The complete set of functions of the package and the corresponding detailed description is available in Cran.[1]

The only input required for the algorithm to run is the commuting flows matrix, the initial parameters (size and self-containment as presented in Chapter 4) and information on the type of coding system used for the basic territorial units (those for whom the commuting data is available).

An example of an LMA delineation process

The LMA delineation process may comprise of the following stages:

1. Preliminary treatment: the algorithm identifies basic territorial units (communities) presenting anomalies (only incoming or outgoing or internal flows) and provides a report of such features in the data (function *findClusters*).

2. Regionalisation algorithm: this is the core of the package and it is dealt with by the function *findCluster*. This function implements a greedy algorithm to aggregate the basic territorial units into clusters and find the territorial partition representing the LMAs. Starting from the basic territorial units, the algorithm iteratively aggregates them until all clusters satisfy the validity criteria (Annex A) set by the validity function and the parameters. Figure A C.1 presents a schematic workflow of the algorithm. A very basic application of the algorithm is given below:

   ```
   library(LabourMarketAreas)
   
   ##read commuting flows data
   
   dat=fread("commuting flows.txt")
   
   ##apply the iterative algorithm
   
   out<- findClusters(LWCom=dat,minSZ=1000,minSC=0.6667,tarSZ=1000,tarSC=0.75)
   
   ## the object out contains all the information on the set of LMAs found by the algorithm.
   
   ## To view how the basic territorial units have been grouped type:
   
   out$lma$clusterList.
   ```

3. Naming and visualisation of the LMAs: LMAs are named after the community having the maximum incoming flows. When community geographical co-ordinates are available in geospatial vector format (.shp files), tools to deploy this information

at LMA level are included in the package in order to produce LMAs shapefiles and visualise the obtained geography (the function involved are *AssignLmaName* and *CreateLMAShape*).

The figure below illustrates the implementation of the R package LabourMarketAreas.

Figure A C.1. Scheme of the implementation of the R package LabourMarketAreas

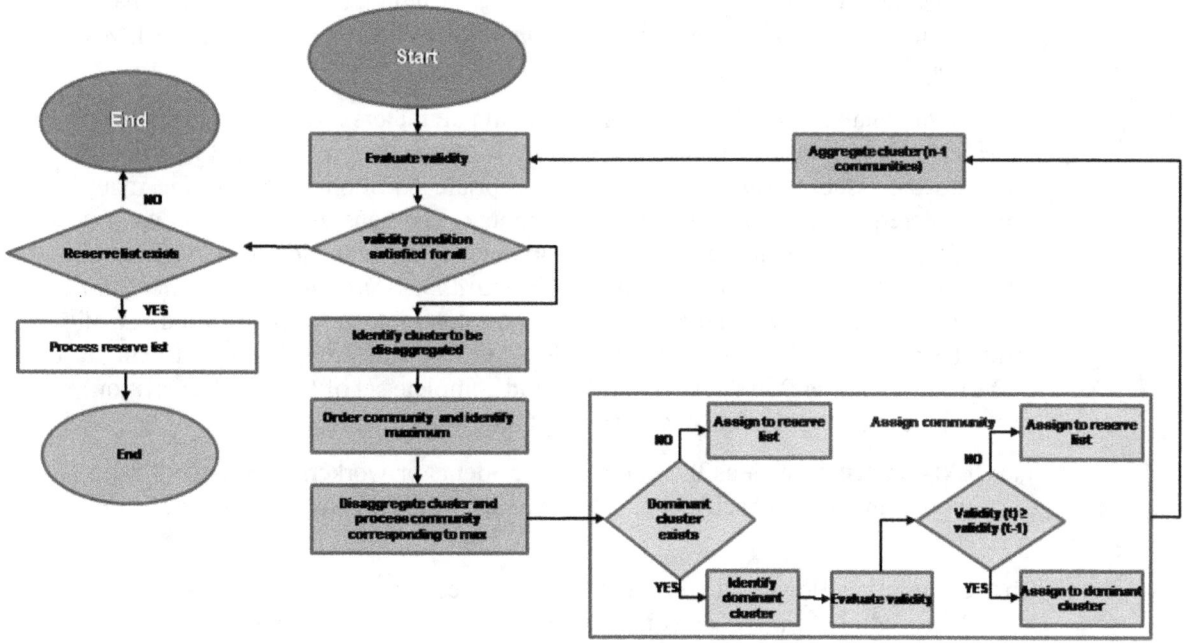

Source: Derived from Istat, 2014: https://www.istat.it/it/archivio/142676.

4. Fine-tuning of the geography: As the algorithm is based exclusively on commuting flows, some areas may include communities not spatially contiguous. Based on geospatial information, the tools implemented in the R package allow complying with the contiguity principle. This stage of the process is performed in an interactive manner, as expert knowledge has to be exploited to assign correctly communities to labour market areas. Four distinct functions implement the fine-tuning process, namely: *CreateLMAShape*, *FindIsolated*, *FindContig* and *AssignSingleComToSingleLma*. These functions respectively create the LMA geospatial vector, find the isolated territorial units one after the other, propose the possible LMAs that are contiguous to the isolated territorial unit under examination and assign the latter to the one selected by the user. A schematic application of this principle is given below:

shape_terr_unit=rgdal::readOGR(dsn = "my_directory" layer = "BasicTerritorial_Units_shape_file")

*shape_lma=**CreateLMAShape**(lma=out$lma,shp_com=shape_terr_unit, ...)*

*iso=**FindIsolated**(lma=out$lma, lma_shp=shape_lma$shp_lma, com_shp=shape_terr_unit, ...)*

> *conti.lma=**FindContig**(type="lma",lma=out$lma,contig.matrix=iso$isolated.lma$contig.matrix.lma,*
> *isolated=iso$isolated.lma$lma.unique$lma.unique.ID)*
>
> *out_1=**AssignSingleComToSingleLma**(out$lma,names(conti.lma)[1],conti.lma[[1]],dat).*

5. Comparison of possible alternative LMAs in a given area of the country; to analyse the coherence, consistency and appropriateness of individual allocations of basic territorial units, the function *PlotLmaCommunity* compares two candidate LMA partitions containing the specified territorial units.

6. Sensitivity analysis: Different sets of the initial parameters imply slightly different LMA configurations; the investigation of such geographies is essential in order to address the issue of finding the most appropriate partition satisfying the many different requirements needed by each country. The sensitivity analysis can be performed by setting different groups of parameters in the function *findClusters* and collecting the results. The functions *CompareLMAsStat* and *StatClusterData* enable the quantitative analysis of the output stemming from a specified set of initial parameters. These functions provide statistics on different dimensions: single LMAs, commuting flows between LMAs and complete set of LMAs (the partition) as a whole. Examples of such statistics pertain:

    a. LMA statistics such as the number of residents or workers, home-work ratio, supply and demand self-containment values, internal cohesion link and flows, etc.

    b. Commuting flows statistics such as the percentage of flows below a given threshold, descriptive statistics on incoming or outgoing flows, identification of the LMAs reaching the minimum or maximum incoming or outgoing flows, etc.

    c. Quality statistics on the partition such as the number of clusters, descriptive statistics on supply and demand self-containment, descriptive statistics on number of residents, workers or resident workers, Q-modularity index, etc.

    An example of the use of the function *StatClusterData* is:

    > *Stats = StatClusterData(outlma,outparam,1000,dat)*

7. Further analysis: Further analysis is possible, such as the analysis of the reserve list i.e. those basic territorial units not assigned during the aggregation process to avoid damaging the already existing clusters. The function *StatReserveList* produces statistics on the components.

8. Dissemination: The release of a geography implies the dissemination of a series of products that enable users to both understand and make use of it. Besides the table of correspondence between the basic territorial units (usually municipalities) and the corresponding LMA (provided by *outlmaclusterList*), the geospatial vectors allowing their cartographic representation and some descriptive statistics are usually released coupled with socioeconomic indicators at the LMA level. The function *AddStatistics* joins directly the LMA structure to the desired statistics to ease their further usage and representation. The guidelines2 provide further directions on possible products to be made available.

9. Updating of the geography: The demography of the basic territorial units (fusion of municipalities, changes in their territories, etc.) in some cases may cause the change of the LMA borders. Treatments of these cases need to be addressed in order to keep the different levels of the geographies coherent.

The software modularity has the advantage that new elements can be added quite easily in the package. Further developments are already foreseen at the time of writing.

Notes

[1] https://cran.r-project.org/web/packages/LabourMarketAreas/LabourMarketAreas.pdf.

[2] https://ec.europa.eu/eurostat/cros/system/files/guidelines_for_lmas_production08082017_rev300817.pdf.

Annex D. Self-contained labour areas (SLA-ZTA) – Python package

The Python package SLA-ZTA (for self-contained labour areas – *zones de travail autonomes*) was created to offer an open-source solution to a computational code originally coded in SAS®, and in so doing increase usability, adaptability and transferability of this methodology. Currently, the SLA-ZTA system code is released and maintained as part of a PyPI repository that can be accessed at https://pypi.org/project/SLAZTA/.

The methodology embedded in the SLA-ZTA code reflects a multidirectional-based approach to the delineation of functional areas. The computational core draws largely from the analysis of travel to work (TTW) areas of Britain (Coombes and Bond, 2008[1]), and the code was used to delineate functional areas outside major metropolitan areas in Canada. More details on the data source, geographic unit of analysis and results for Canada were discussed in Chapter 5.

The SLA-ZTA Python code is organised into six core modules, providing adaptability and the possibility to finetune the specifications as required for various applications. The approach underpinning this model is particularly suitable for the delineation of functional areas in what would be generally considered rural or non-metro areas as the clustering procedure puts an emphasis on the strength of commuting flows and, in the existing specification of the model, does not impose a minimum population size for each cluster.

The computational workflow from input matrices to the results generated by the model can be summarised as follows:

1. To create the SLA clusters, the commuting data (Non-symmetric Matrix Flow) is initially reconfigured into a set of data matrices that, for each area, expresses a measure of "success" of self-containment of the labour force, which will be further explained below, and the relationships between that area and every other area with which it shares a commuting relationship (Symmetric Strength Matrix). After this reconfiguration of the databases, the code completes module one to check if all areas have achieved success. If not, the workflow moves to the second module and continues.

2. The code then determines which area is currently farthest away from achieving success. As this method is aimed at discovering non-metropolitan areas, no minimum population size is required to achieve success. Success is defined as the area reaching the level of self-containment desired for its population size and number of employed workers, with that being a sliding scale between 75% self-containment for larger areas and 90% self-containment for smaller areas.

3. For the least successful area, the code then determines the other area with which it shares the strongest reciprocal connection. This is done using the following equation:

$$(F_{a,b})/R_a * (F_{a,b})/W_b + (F_{b,a})/R_b * (F_{b,a})/W_a$$

where Fa,b is the number of journeys to work from area A to area B; Ra is the number of workers who live in area A; and Wa is the number of people who work in area A.

4. The least successful area is joined to the area with which it has the strongest connection, creating a new area.

5. The success metrics (Success Table) and commuting relationships (Symmetric Strength Matrix) are recalculated to include connections between the new area and the remaining areas. Information on previously existing areas (e.g. previous configurations of the data) is discarded at this step in the programme. This ensures that the amount of memory used decreases rather than increases as the programme runs, allowing for much larger data sets to be processed.

6. The code begins again at step 1 and repeats the process until all areas have achieved self-containment; that is, it repeats until all areas are included in the Success Table.

Figure A D.1 provides an overview of the above process.

Figure A D.1. Scheme of the computational flow implemented by the Python package SLA-ZTA

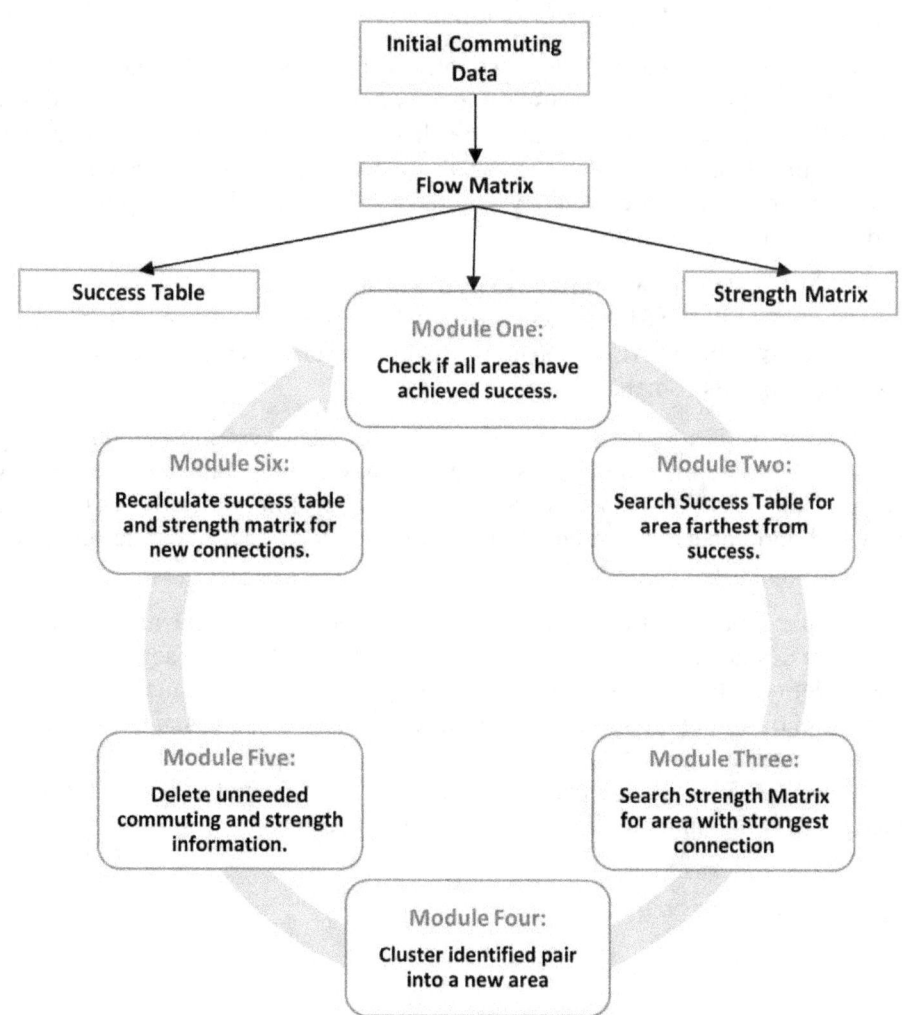

Source: Provided by Statistics Canada, 2019.

After the above clustering process has been completed, a number of areas will usually remain unassigned. These are either areas that are self-contained without clustering or areas for which no commuting information is present or available.

A secondary programmatic process is run to deal with these unassigned areas and to modify the existing SLAs, where necessary, to ensure a set of geographically contiguous and logical areas that cover the whole set of areas. For the Canadian specification, this was done using a ruleset based on the rules already in use by the CMA/CA delineation process. This secondary process is not available in the Python package as it makes extensive use of the Canadian Statistical Geographic Classification system and would currently be unsuitable for use on other data.

When compared to the results of the R package LabourMarketAreas (LMA), it was found that the two systems produce largely comparable results for Canada when the same parameters are given to both systems. There are three major differences between the programmes that can affect the results that are produced:

1. The LMA system excludes municipalities that do not have both in and out commuting data. The degree of impact that this has on the data will depend on the suppression procedures that are used and the frequency with which this situation occurs in the area of interest.

2. The two systems select areas in slightly different ways, with the LMA system selecting areas with the lowest self-containment and the SLA system selecting areas with the farthest distance to go to reach success. Because smaller areas have a higher threshold to reach for success, this means that smaller areas will tend to be chosen first more often even when their overall level of self-containment is identical to larger areas.

3. The LMA system allows clusters to be dissolved if they are still not successful after clustering, while the SLA system does not. This is a methodological difference due to the focus of the SLA areas on non-metropolitan areas where the choice of pairing areas can be quite small.

Because of the above issues, there is a tendency for the SLA system to produce a slightly greater number of areas than the LMA system when the same parameters are used. Apart from the exclusions mentioned above in point 1, this reflects minor differences in how areas are subdivided and appears to be largely due to the SLA system being designed to find small functional areas where possible.

Finally, it should be recalled that the Canadian self-contained labour areas presented in Chapter 5 were designed from their formation to complement the already existing system of Census Metropolitan Areas and Census Agglomerations. Because of that, some programmatic choices and the specification of threshold values were adapted to the specific need to create usable non-metropolitan functional areas. Applications to other national contexts of the SLA-ZTA Python package have been implemented as part of this research undertaking, with minimum modifications of the package.

Annex E. Sensitivity of functional areas to parameter specification

The following section provides a sensitivity analysis of functional areas to different parameters specification for the countries where the methodology was applied.

Table A E.1. Sensitivity analysis, Canada

Scenario	W_{min} (000s)	W_{target} (000s)	SC_{min} (%)	SC_{target} (%)	Without CMA		With CMA	
					Number of areas	Average population	Number of areas	Average population
1	0	50	0.80	0.95	351	15.7	225	155.8
2	0	40	0.80	0.95	353	15.6	232	151.1
3	0	50	0.75	0.95	354	15.6	238	147.2
4	0	40	0.75	0.95	359	15.3	245	143.0
5	0	25	0.80	0.95	364	15.2	247	141.9
6	0	15	0.80	0.95	378	14.5	268	130.7
7	0	25	0.75	0.95	369	14.9	271	129.2
8	0	15	0.75	0.95	382	14.3	285	122.9
9	0	50	0.75	0.90	421	12.9	309	113.2
10	0	40	0.75	0.90	423	12.9	315	111.5
11	0	5	0.80	0.95	410	13.2	317	110.4
12	0	25	0.75	0.90	428	12.7	323	108.3
13	0	15	0.75	0.90	440	12.3	337	103.8
14	0	50	0.60	0.90	428	12.7	338	103.4
15	0	5	0.75	0.95	431	12.6	342	102.3
16	0	40	0.60	0.90	434	12.4	346	101.1
17	0	25	0.60	0.90	447	12.1	366	95.5
18	0	5	0.75	0.90	483	11.2	376	92.9
19	0	50	0.65	0.85	488	11.0	385	90.7
20	0	15	0.60	0.90	463	11.7	391	89.4
21	0	40	0.65	0.85	489	10.9	391	89.3
22	0	25	0.65	0.85	495	10.8	401	87.1
23	0	15	0.65	0.85	508	10.5	413	84.5
24	0	5	0.65	0.85	534	9.8	450	77.5
25	0	5	0.60	0.90	512	10.4	451	77.4

Note: The table above shows the results using different parameters. The columns W_{min} and W_{target} specify the minimum and target number of employees in thousands respectively. The columns SC_{min} and SC_{target} specify the minimum and target levels of self-containment in percentages respectively. Number of areas denotes the total number of clusters for a given scenario. Avg. units per cluster denotes the mean number of geographic units contained in each cluster. Average size denotes the average number of employees per cluster. FUA included denotes if the municipalities that form part of a functional urban area were included in the calculation. The table summarises the results before post-processing.
Source: Calculations provided by Statistics Canada.

Table A E.2. Sensitivity analysis, United States

Scenario	W_{min} (000s)	W_{target} (000s)	SC_{min} (%)	SC_{target} (%)	Number of areas	Avg. units per cluster	Average size: employees	FUA included
1	50	100	65	85	327	7	265 320	No
2	50	100	65	85	512	6	635 348	Yes
3	50	100	70	95	298	8	291 139	No
4	50	100	70	95	451	7	721 282	Yes
5	50	100	75	90	301	8	288 237	No
6	50	100	75	90	414	8	785 744	Yes
7	50	150	65	85	322	8	269 439	No
8	50	150	65	85	473	7	687 734	Yes
9	50	150	70	95	278	9	312 084	No
10	50	150	70	95	405	8	803 205	Yes
11	50	150	75	90	289	8	300 206	No
12	50	150	75	90	384	8	847 131	Yes
13	50	200	65	85	314	8	276 304	No
14	50	200	65	85	452	7	719 686	Yes
15	50	200	70	95	265	9	327 394	No
16	50	200	70	95	374	9	869 781	Yes
17	50	200	75	90	281	9	308 753	No
18	50	200	75	90	370	9	879 184	Yes
19	100	200	65	85	180	13	481 997	No
20	100	200	65	85	358	9	908 654	Yes
21	100	200	70	95	162	15	535 552	No
22	100	200	70	95	321	10	1 013 390	Yes
23	100	200	75	90	165	15	525 815	No
24	100	200	75	90	299	11	1 087 954	Yes
25	100	300	65	85	176	14	492 952	No
26	100	300	65	85	339	9	959 582	Yes
27	100	300	70	95	152	16	570 786	No
28	100	300	70	95	282	11	1 153 540	Yes
29	100	300	75	90	157	15	552 608	No
30	100	300	75	90	273	12	1 191 568	Yes

Note: The table above shows the results using different parameters. The columns W_{min} and W_{target} specify the minimum and target number of employees in thousands respectively. The columns SC_{min} and SC_{target} specify the minimum and target levels of self-containment in percentages respectively. *Number of areas* denotes the total number of clusters for a given scenario. *Avg. units per cluster* denotes the mean number of geographic units contained in each cluster. *Average size* denotes the average number of employees per cluster. *FUA included* denotes if the municipalities that form part of a functional urban area were included in the calculation. The table summarises the results before post-processing.

Table A E.3. Sensitivity of results excluding FUAs, Mexico

Scenario	W_{min} (000s)	W_{target} (000s)	SC_{min} (%)	SC_{target} (%)	Number of areas	Avg. units per cluster	Average size: employees	FUA included
1	50	100	65	85	141	14	320 702	No
2	50	100	65	85	207	12	612 004	Yes
3	50	100	70	95	135	15	334 955	No
4	50	100	70	95	193	13	656 398	Yes
5	50	100	75	90	136	15	332 492	No
6	50	100	75	90	186	13	681 102	Yes
7	50	150	65	85	141	14	320 702	No
8	50	150	65	85	200	12	633 424	Yes
9	50	150	70	95	133	15	339 992	No
10	50	150	70	95	176	14	719 801	Yes
11	50	150	75	90	136	15	332 492	No
12	50	150	75	90	176	14	719 801	Yes
13	50	200	65	85	141	14	320 702	No
14	50	200	65	85	196	12	646 352	Yes
15	50	200	70	95	132	15	342 568	No
16	50	200	70	95	171	14	740 847	Yes
17	50	200	75	90	135	15	334 955	No
18	50	200	75	90	176	14	719 801	Yes
19	100	200	65	85	69	29	655 347	No
20	100	200	65	85	125	20	1 013 479	Yes
21	100	200	70	95	70	28	645 984	No
22	100	200	70	95	120	20	1 055 707	Yes
23	100	200	75	90	68	29	664 984	No
24	100	200	75	90	116	21	1 092 111	Yes
25	100	300	65	85	69	29	655 347	No
26	100	300	65	85	120	20	1 055 707	Yes

Note: The table above shows the results using different parameters. The columns W_{min} and W_{target} specify the minimum and target number of employees in thousands respectively. The columns SC_{min} and SC_{target} specify the minimum and target levels of self-containment in percentages respectively. *Number of areas* denotes the total number of clusters for a given scenario. *Avg. units per cluster* denotes the mean number of geographic units contained in each cluster. *Average size* denotes the average number of employees per cluster. *FUA included* denotes if the municipalities that form part of a functional urban area were included in the calculation. The table summarises the results before post-processing.

Table A E.4. Sensitivity analysis, Estonia

Scenario	W_{min} (000s)	W_{target} (000s)	SC_{min} (%)	SC_{target} (%)	Number of areas	Avg. units per cluster	Avg. size	FUA included
1	1	2	70	95	27	31	51 765	Yes
2	1	2	75	90	19	44	73 560	Yes
3	1	3	75	90	19	44	73 560	Yes
4	1	4	75	90	19	44	73 560	Yes
5	10	20	65	85	15	45	38 676	No
6	10	20	65	85	20	42	69 882	Yes
7	10	20	70	95	14	48	41 439	No
8	10	20	70	95	16	53	87 353	Yes
9	10	20	75	90	13	52	44 627	No
10	10	20	75	90	13	65	107 511	Yes
11	10	30	65	85	13	52	44 627	No
12	10	30	65	85	15	56	93 176	Yes
13	10	30	70	95	12	56	48 345	No
14	10	30	70	95	11	77	127 059	Yes
15	10	30	75	90	11	61	52 740	No
16	10	30	75	90	10	85	139 765	Yes
17	10	40	65	85	11	61	52 740	No
18	10	40	65	85	13	65	107 511	Yes
19	10	40	70	95	9	75	64 461	No
20	10	40	70	95	9	94	155 294	Yes
21	10	40	75	90	10	67	58 015	No
22	10	40	75	90	9	94	155 294	Yes
23	50	100	65	85	4	169	145 036	No
24	50	100	65	85	6	141	232 941	Yes
25	50	100	70	95	4	169	145 036	No
26	50	100	70	95	5	169	279 529	Yes
27	50	100	75	90	2	337	290 073	No
28	50	100	75	90	5	169	279 529	Yes
29	50	150	65	85	5	135	116 029	No
30	50	150	65	85	6	141	232 941	Yes
31	50	150	70	95	2	337	290 073	No
32	50	150	70	95	3	282	465 882	Yes
33	50	150	75	90	2	337	290 073	No
34	50	150	75	90	5	169	279 529	Yes
35	50	200	65	85	3	225	193 382	No
36	50	200	65	85	5	169	279 529	Yes
37	50	200	70	95	2	337	290 073	No
38	50	200	70	95	3	282	465 882	Yes
39	50	200	75	90	2	337	290 073	No
40	50	200	75	90	4	211	349 411	Yes

Note: The table above shows the results using different parameters. The columns W_{min} and W_{target} specify the minimum and target number of employees in thousands respectively. The columns SC_{min} and SC_{target} specify the minimum and target levels of self-containment in percentages respectively. *Number of areas* denotes the total number of clusters for a given scenario. *Avg. units per cluster* denotes the mean number of geographic units contained in each cluster. *Average size* denotes the average number of people per cluster. *FUA included* denotes if the municipalities that form part of a functional urban area were included in the calculation. The table summarises the results before post-processing.

Table A E.5. Sensitivity analysis, Korea

Scenario	W_{min} (000s)	W_{target} (000s)	SC_{min} (%)	SC_{target} (%)	Number of areas	Avg. units per cluster	Average size: employees	FUA included
1	50	100	65	85	45	2	158 846	No
2	50	100	65	85	69	3	624 565	Yes
3	50	100	70	95	45	2	158 846	No
4	50	100	70	95	57	4	756 052	Yes
5	50	100	75	90	44	3	162 456	No
6	50	100	75	90	52	4	828 749	Yes
7	50	150	65	85	45	2	158 846	No
8	50	150	65	85	62	4	695 080	Yes
9	50	150	70	95	41	3	174 344	No
10	50	150	70	95	48	5	897 812	Yes
11	50	150	75	90	43	3	166 235	No
12	50	150	75	90	46	5	936 847	Yes
13	50	200	65	85	44	3	162 456	No
14	50	200	65	85	62	4	695 080	Yes
15	50	200	70	95	41	3	174 344	No
16	50	200	70	95	46	5	936 847	Yes
17	50	200	75	90	43	3	166 235	No
18	50	200	75	90	45	5	957 666	Yes
19	100	200	65	85	27	4	264 744	No
20	100	200	65	85	46	5	936 847	Yes
21	100	200	70	95	26	4	274 926	No
22	100	200	70	95	39	6	1 104 999	Yes
23	100	200	75	90	26	4	274 926	No
24	100	200	75	90	38	6	1 134 078	Yes
25	100	300	65	85	27	4	264 744	No
26	100	300	65	85	44	5	979 431	Yes
27	100	300	70	95	26	4	274 926	No
28	100	300	70	95	35	6	1 231 285	Yes
29	100	300	75	90	26	4	274 926	No
30	100	300	75	90	36	6	1 197 083	Yes
31	100	400	65	85	27	4	264 744	No
32	100	400	65	85	44	5	979 431	Yes
33	100	400	70	95	26	4	274 926	No
34	100	400	70	95	33	7	1 305 908	Yes
35	100	400	75	90	26	4	274 926	No
36	100	400	75	90	34	7	1 267 499	Yes
37	200	400	65	85	12	9	595 674	No
38	200	400	65	85	34	7	1 267 499	Yes
39	200	400	70	95	12	9	595 674	No
40	200	400	70	95	29	8	1 486 034	Yes
41	200	400	75	90	12	9	595 674	No
42	200	400	75	90	29	8	1 486 034	Yes

Note: The table above shows the results using different parameters. The columns W_{min} and W_{target} specify the minimum and target number of employees in thousands respectively. The columns SC_{min} and SC_{target} specify the minimum and target levels of self-containment in percentages respectively. *Number of areas* denotes the total number of clusters for a given scenario. *Avg. units per cluster* denotes the mean number of geographic units contained in each cluster. *Average employees* denotes the average number of employees per cluster. *FUA included* denotes if the municipalities that form part of a functional urban area were included in the calculation. The table summarises the results before post-processing.